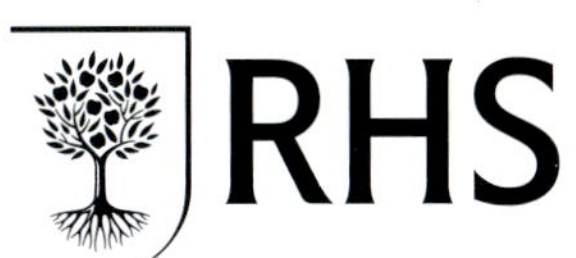 

WILDFLOWERS

THE WATERCOLOUR ART PAD

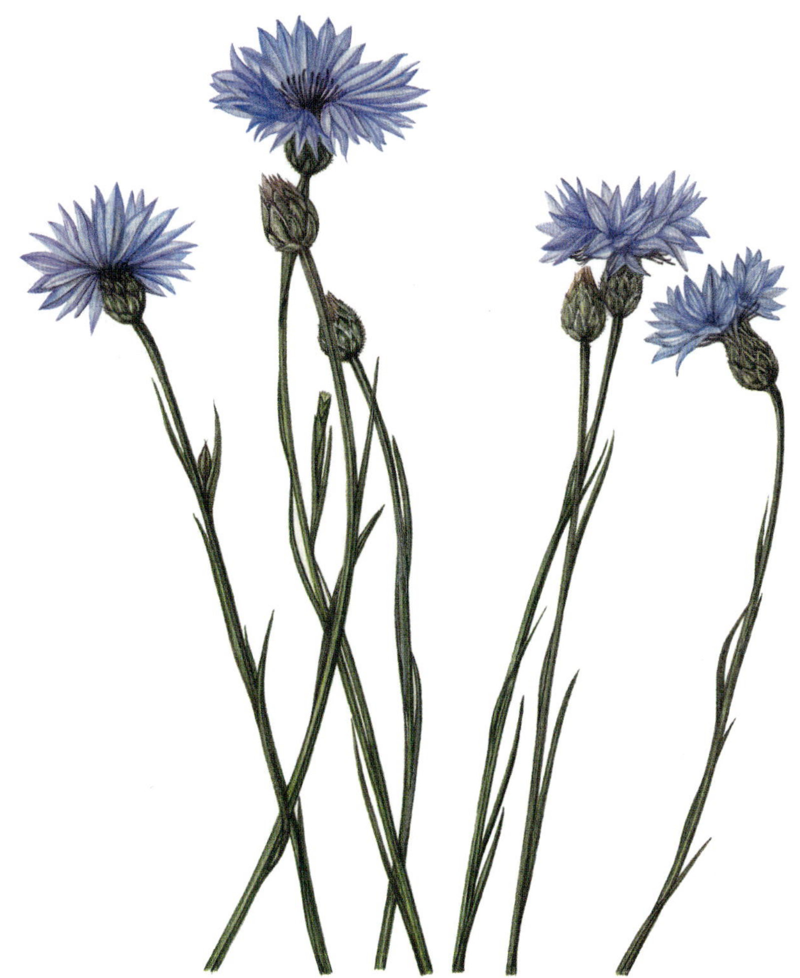

RACHEL PEDDER-SMITH

MITCHELL
BEAZLEY

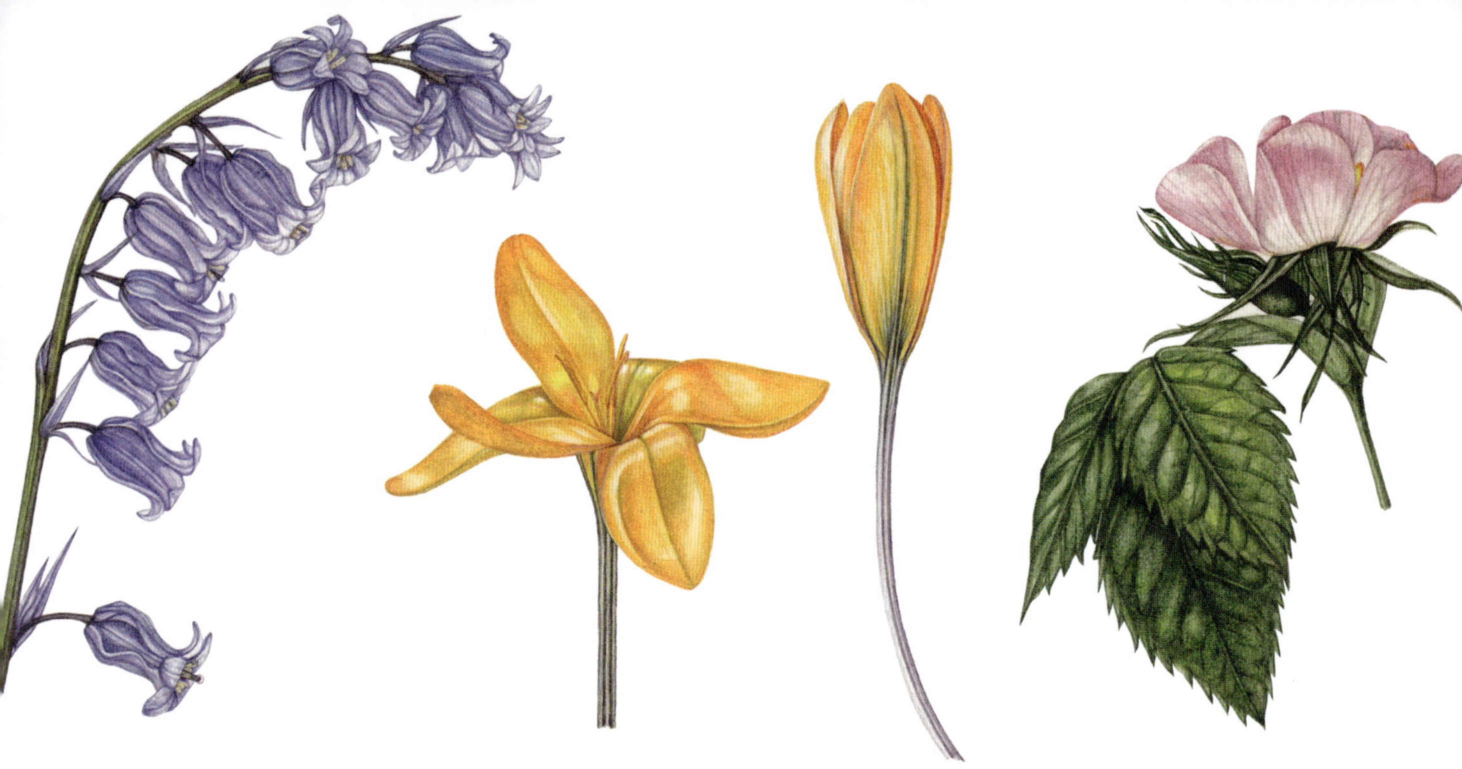

The Royal Horticultural Society is the UK's leading gardening charity dedicated to advancing horticulture and promoting good gardening. Its charitable work includes providing expert advice and information, training the next generation of gardeners, creating hands-on opportunities for children to grow plants, and conducting research into plants, pests and environmental issues affecting gardeners.

For more information, visit www.rhs.org.uk or call 0845 130 4646

First published in Great Britain in 2023 by Mitchell Beazley
a division of Octopus Publishing Group Limited
Carmelite House
50 Victoria Embankment
London EC4Y 0DZ
www.octopusbooks.co.uk

An Hachette UK Company
www.hachette.co.uk

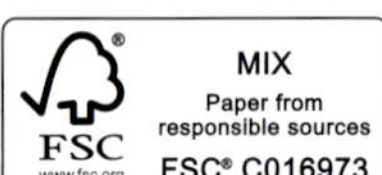

Published in association with the Royal Horticultural Society
Copyright © 2023 Quarto Publishing plc

Distributed in the US by Hachette Book Group
1290 Avenue of the Americas
4th and 5th Floors
New York, NY 10104

Distributed in Canada by Canadian Manda Group
664 Annette St.
Toronto
Ontario
Canada M6S 2C8

A CIP record for this book is available from the British Library

ISBN 978-1-78472-887-8

This book was conceived, designed and produced by
The Bright Press, an imprint of the Quarto Group
1 Triptych Place, London, SE1 9SH
www.Quarto.com

Designer: www.wheeldesign.co.uk
Editors: Anna Southgate and Abbie Sharman
Managing Editor: Jacqui Sayers
Editorial Director: Isheeta Mustafi
Publisher: James Evans
Mitchell Beazley Publisher: Alison Starling
RHS Publisher: Helen Griffin

All illustrations by Rachel Pedder-Smith

10 9 8 7 6 5 4 3 2 1

Printed in China

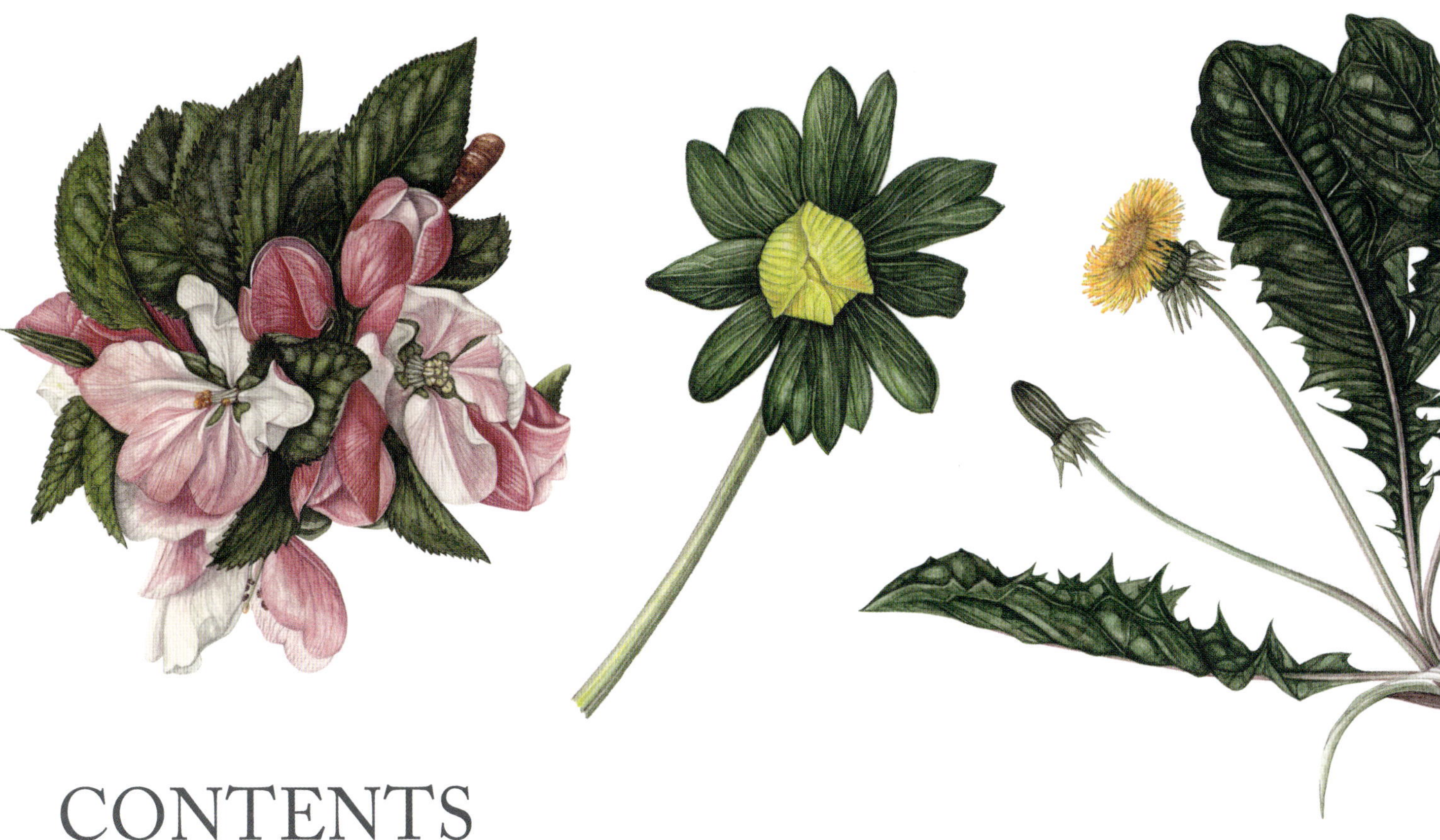

CONTENTS

Get Painting

Turn to the art pad on page 25 and pull out a page to get started.

Introduction

My favourite moment in painting is when the object has been drawn out and I use the wet-on-wet technique (see page 7) to make my first mark. Using clean water, I wet the area I want to colour, mix my first colour wash, drop it onto the damp paper and watch how – as if by magic – the paint spreads to the outer limit of the damp area. This is a captivating moment every time – the first step to creating a new piece of art.

Watercolour has been the traditional medium used for botanical art for a number of reasons. In previous centuries, on voyages of discovery when ships' artists needed to record the exotic plants they saw, they favoured watercolour for its versatility, subtlety and ability to capture the delicate and sometimes ethereal nature of petals. The same is true today, and watercolours are easy to use wherever you are – from your studio or kitchen table to in the field.

To produce good watercolour pieces you do not have to have a massive range of paints; I have a medium-sized travel paint box and regularly rely on 25 different colours. I prefer pans to tubes as I find these more accessible and quick to use, but there is no real difference in the end results. It is important to buy professional quality paints as they have more pigment and are not chalky, unlike student quality watercolours. I use the metal leaves of my paint travel set as a palette and I never wash the colours off, as they often come in useful for another painting. When I get short of space I simply clean off a small section with a tissue.

There are 15 paintings to produce in this book with a full range of textures and weights, from the light and sensitive petals of a dog rose or pink poppy, to the shiny, deep green of the cuckoo pint leaves. I hope you enjoy painting them.

Rachel Pedder-Smith

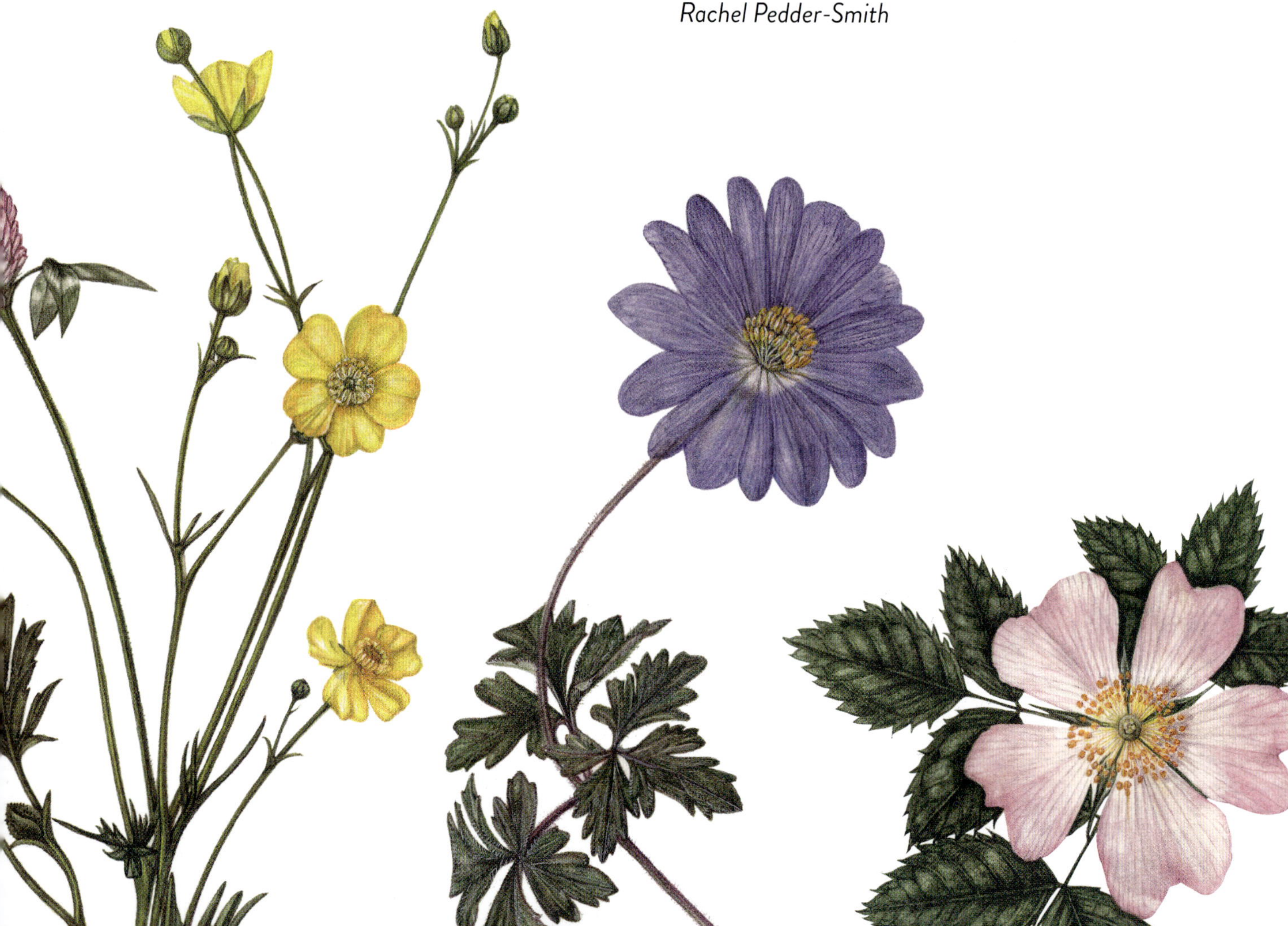

How to use this book

Select a subject
Choose the wildflower you want to paint from the gallery on pages 16–24. Then find the sheet with its printed outline in the art pad section at the back.

Pull out the sheet
Remove the sheet by pressing down on the opposite page and pulling firmly but carefully. Secure it to a surface by taping it down with masking tape along all four edges. This will help to prevent the paper buckling when wet.

Refer to the Gallery
As you paint, refer back to the original artwork and the recommended colour palettes in the gallery.

Advice for beginners
For guidance on how to get started with watercolours, turn to page 6. As well as describing the equipment you'll need, it shows the full palette of colours used in this book, with their names and key numbers. Before you embark on your first project, using spare paper, practise the watercolour techniques described on page 7 and try the tutorials on the pages that follow. When it comes to painting the flowers, you will find that some of the finer details have been simplified in the line artwork, allowing you the freedom to add more or less detail, as you wish.

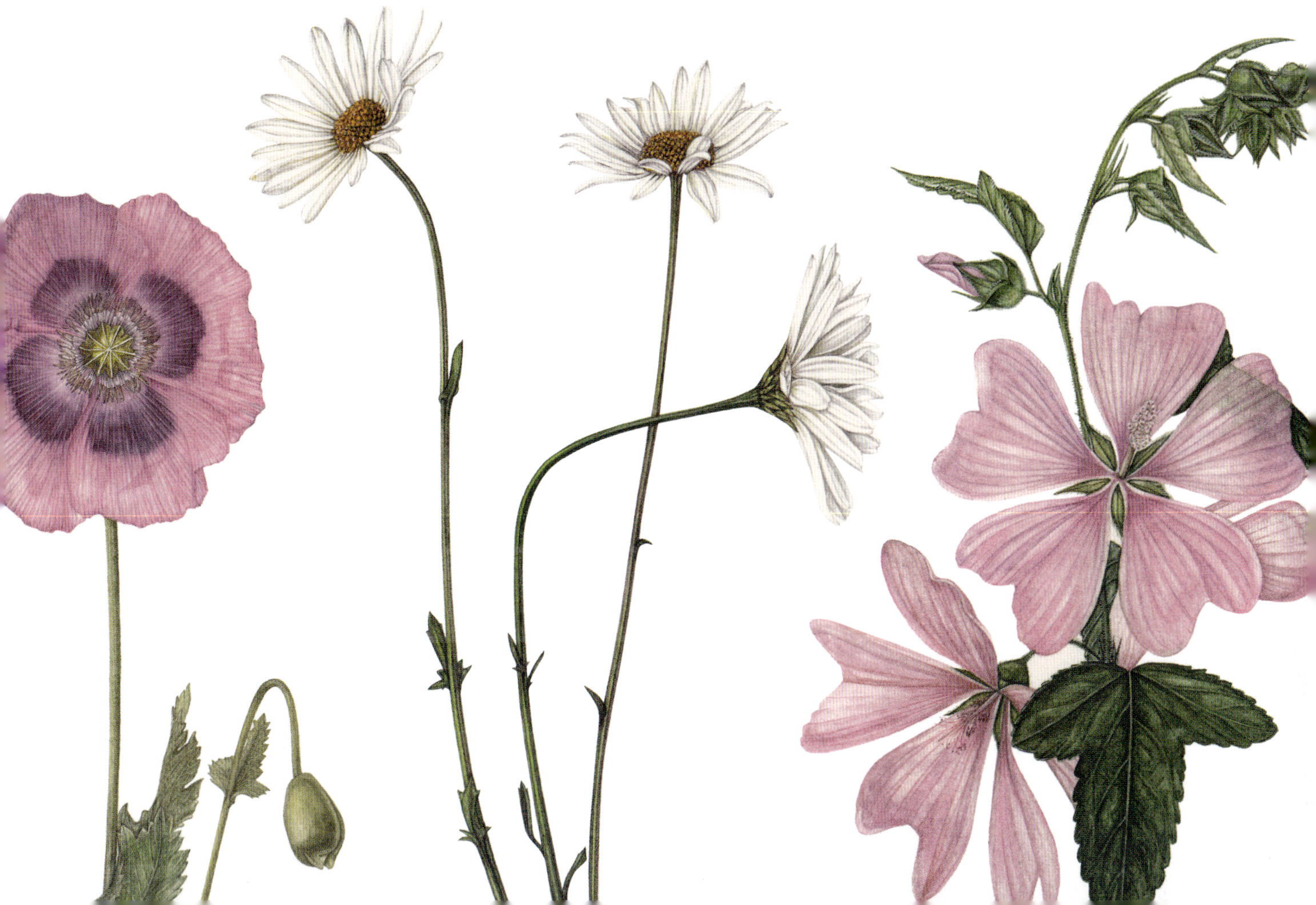

Getting started

Flower painter's toolkit

Before you embark on your adventure as a watercolour flower painter, you'll need to have some basic kit. Listed here are the essential tools and materials you'll need to recreate the botanical paintings in this book.

Paints

For rich, jewel-like colour, it's important to use professional-quality paints, as these contain more pigment. You can buy them in tubes or pans (little blocks); pans have the advantage of being easy and quick to work with. The paintings in this book require 19 different colours – you can see them listed on the right. In some cases you may have to combine many colours to create the right one for a particular petal.

Palette

The metal leaves of a travel paint set make a very handy palette, and it's a good idea never to wash the colours off as you may find yourself using them on another day. If you start to run short of space, just clean off a small section. If you don't have a purpose-made palette, you could use a white ceramic plate instead.

Brushes

You'll need four sizes of paintbrush: a size 6, a size 4, a size 000 and a size 0000. These are a synthetic and sable mix and keep their fine point for longer than pure sable; they are also more reasonably priced. The largest brush is ideal for the initial washes and the smaller brushes can be used for all of the detail, reserving the size 0000 for fine lines.

Paper towels

It is essential to have a tissue or paper towels to hand as you paint. You'll find you use them frequently, whether to wipe colour off the brush when using a dry-brush technique, to create highlights by lifting colour off the paper, or to remove colour immediately if you make a mistake.

Masking fluid

This can be useful for masking out small, precise areas that you want to retain as highlights. It comes in bottles, or in a handy pen form that allows you to apply the fluid directly via the nib. If applying with a brush, dip the brush into a detergent solution first and wipe off the excess moisture with paper towels before dipping it into the fluid, to prevent clogging. Allow the fluid to dry completely before painting over it.

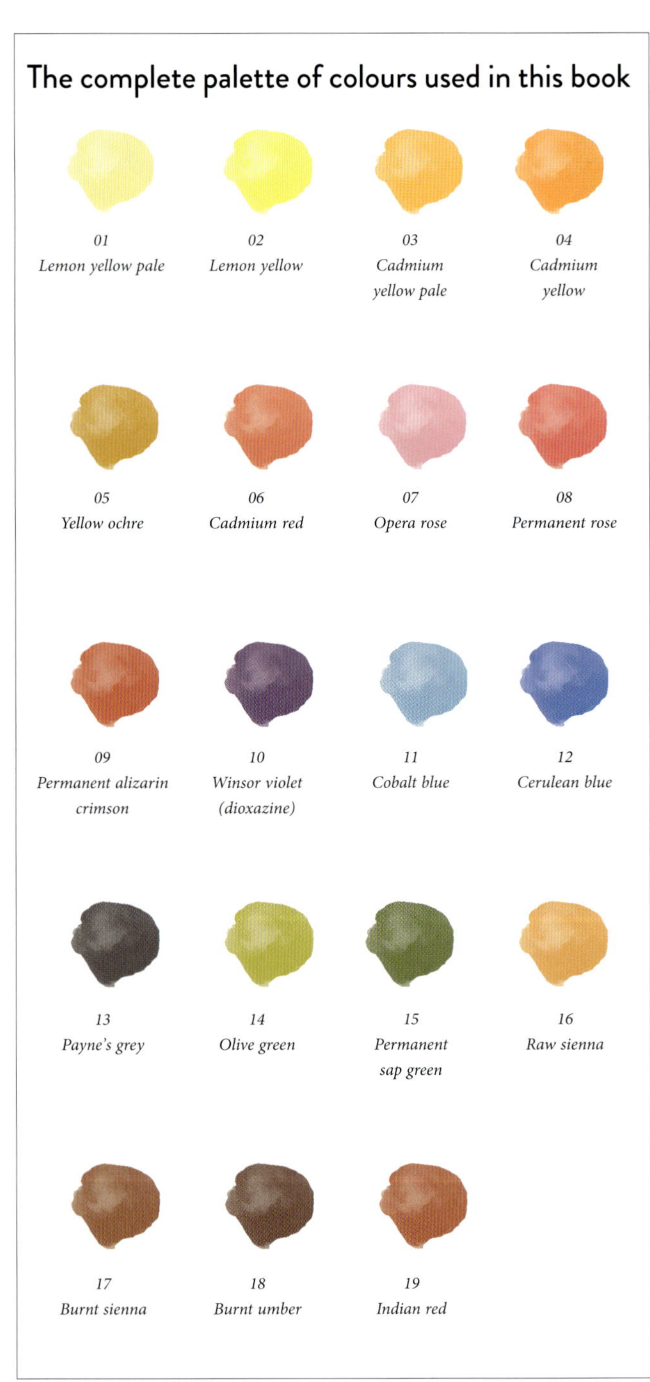

The complete palette of colours used in this book

01 *Lemon yellow pale*	*02* *Lemon yellow*	*03* *Cadmium yellow pale*	*04* *Cadmium yellow*
05 *Yellow ochre*	*06* *Cadmium red*	*07* *Opera rose*	*08* *Permanent rose*
09 *Permanent alizarin crimson*	*10* *Winsor violet (dioxazine)*	*11* *Cobalt blue*	*12* *Cerulean blue*
13 *Payne's grey*	*14* *Olive green*	*15* *Permanent sap green*	*16* *Raw sienna*
17 *Burnt sienna*	*18* *Burnt umber*	*19* *Indian red*	

Watercolour terms and techniques

There are a few key watercolour techniques that you'll return to again and again on the different projects in this book. Try them out on spare paper first so that you really get to know how to use them.

Making a wash

Watercolour paint needs to be mixed with water to liquefy it. The more water you add, the thinner the mixture will be and the lighter the colour. This combination of paint and water is known as a 'wash'. Dip your brush into water and then load it with your desired colour. Use your palette to adjust the balance of colour to water or to mix with other colours.

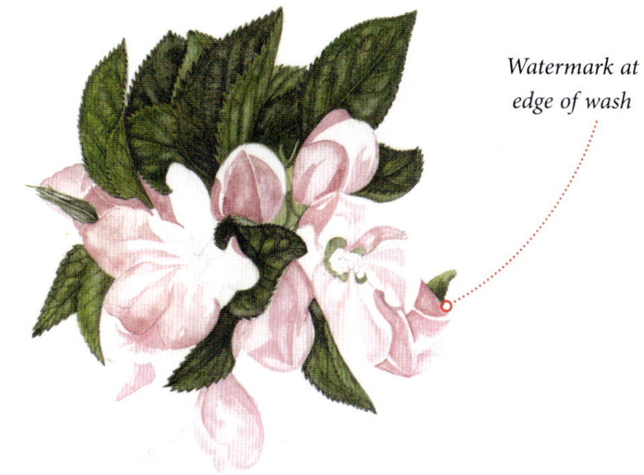

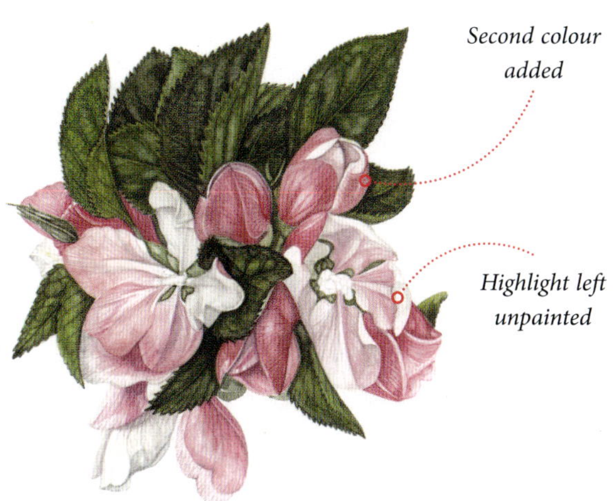

Painting wet-on-wet

Used only when applying the first wash, this technique involves painting onto wet paper or paint. First, wet the paper using a large brush and clean water. Take it only as far as you want the colour to spread and leave highlighted areas dry. Now apply the first wash of colour with a large brush and watch the paint flow evenly over the wet surface to the edge, where it will stop, leaving a distinct line or watermark. You can add in different colours while still wet.

Painting wet-on-dry

For this technique, you wait for the previous layer of paint to dry before applying the next. Use this method to build up the colour after applying the first wash. Working on a dry surface gives greater control over the spread of the paint. Use a large brush to apply the wash to the dry paper in certain areas, building up the colour, shading and giving loose definition to the petals.

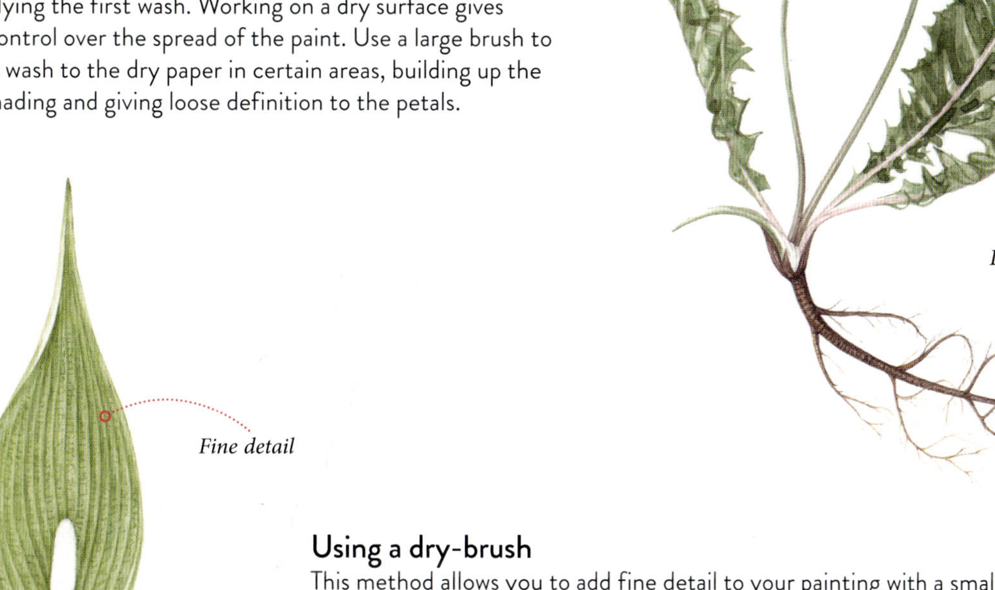

Using a dry-brush

This method allows you to add fine detail to your painting with a small brush – using the brush almost like a pencil. Dip the brush into the paint regularly, but wipe it carefully on some paper towels to remove any excess colour before touching the paper. Use the dry-brush technique to build up texture with fine lines and tiny vein details.

How to paint flowers with fleshy petals

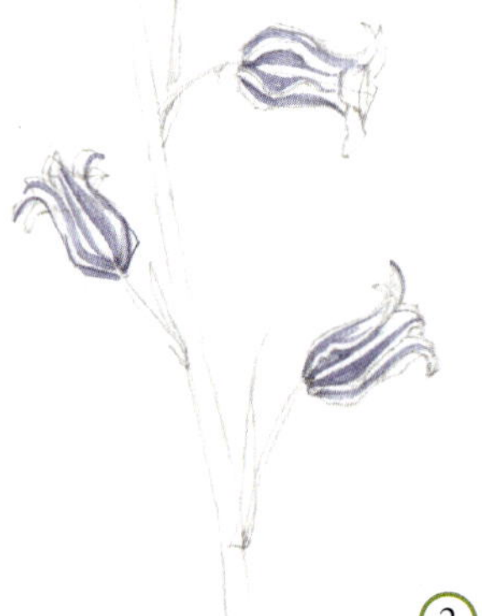

I have chosen bluebells for this tutorial as they have great texture. The colour fades from violet to almost white, with a noticeable stripe. On flowers with fleshy petals, the trick is to capture the way in which the petals turn over and fold back on themselves.

1 Painting the flowers

Mix a thick wash of cobalt blue with a little violet. Use this to paint the darkest blue parts of each flower. Start at the base, where the petals overlap, and make long brushstrokes that follow the form to the tip.

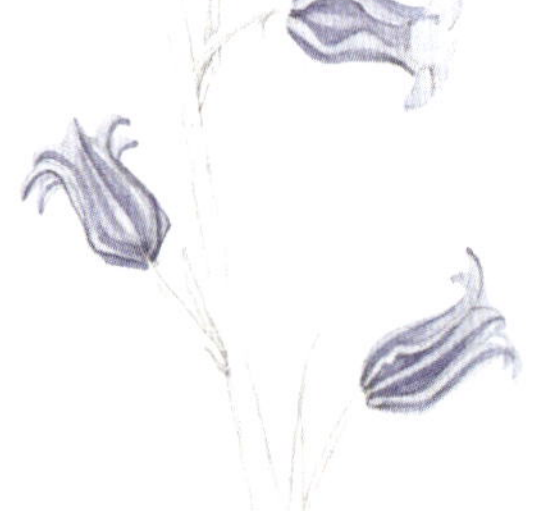 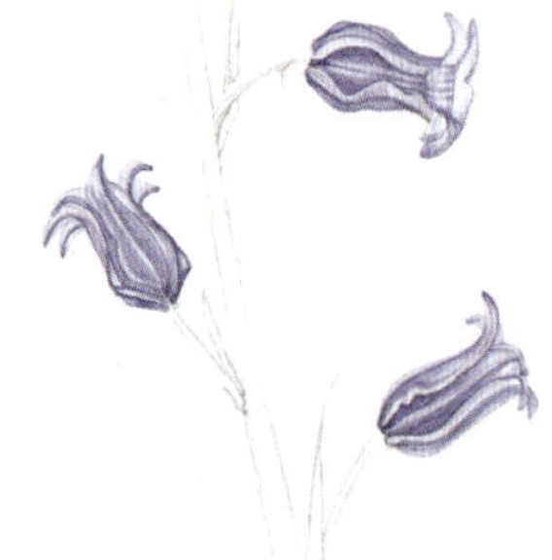 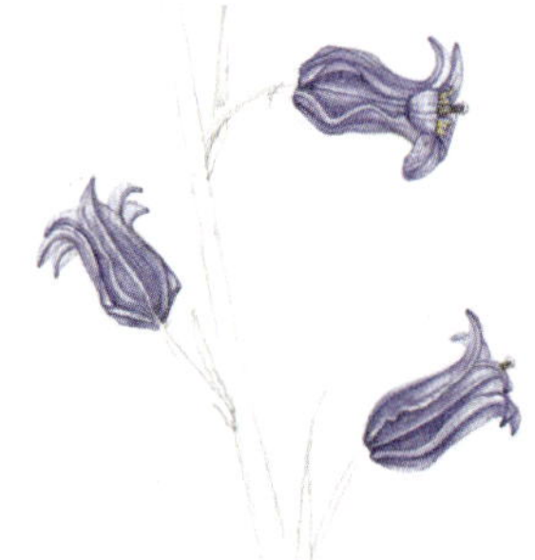

2 Use clear water to pull the colour into the main body of the flower to create lighter sections. Use clear water alone to 'colour' the petals where they are almost white.

3 Return to your first wash to refine the darkest areas of blue. Take care to retain the fine white lines at the edges of the petals, as this will help to show that they are soft and fleshy.

4 Still using the dark wash, add small lines to the surface of the petals to show their fleshy structure. Use a sap green wash for the stigma, with a touch of violet on the very end. Use lemon yellow pale for the anthers. Darken the blue behind the anthers.

5 Follow steps 1–4 to work up the colour on the mid-stem flowers. Repeat to work up the colour on the uppermost flowers.

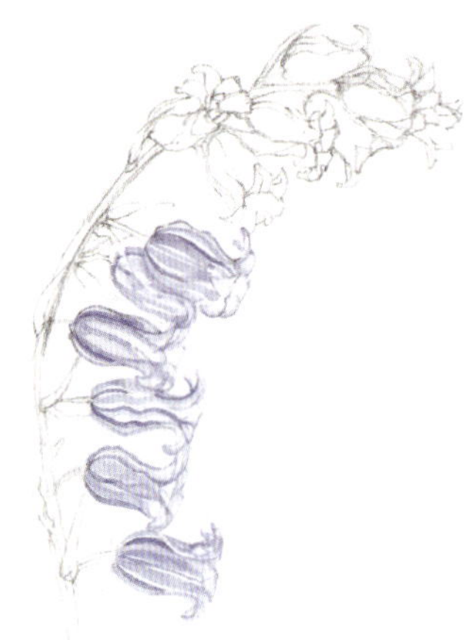 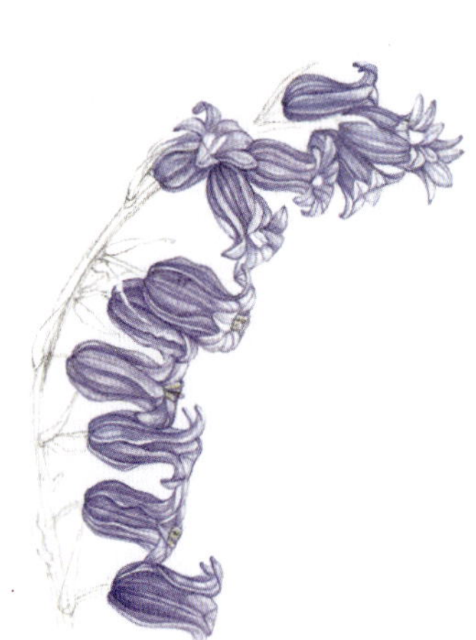

6 **Paint the sepals**

Combine cobalt blue and violet to create a light purple wash for the sepals. Use a fluid brushstroke to work from the bottom of each to its thinner top.

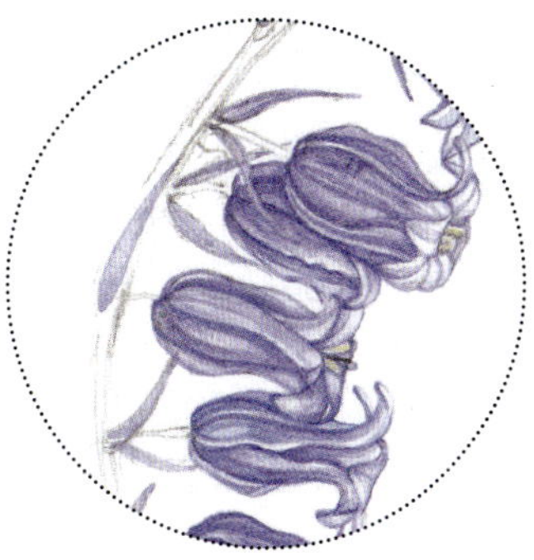

7 Darken the cobalt blue/violet wash and add a stripe down the centre of each sepal. Darken the base and any areas that are shadow.

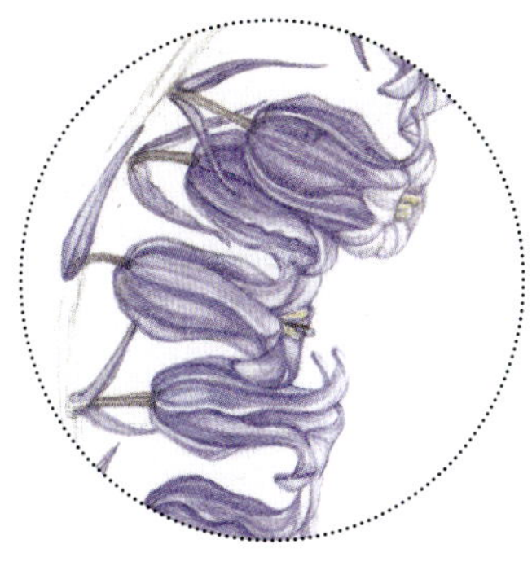

8 **Paint the stems**

For the main stem, mix sap green into the purple wash to make a dark green, and apply to one edge of the stem.

9 Use the sap green/purple wash for the flower stems of the bells; paint dark lines along the edges and use clear water to pull colour into the middle.

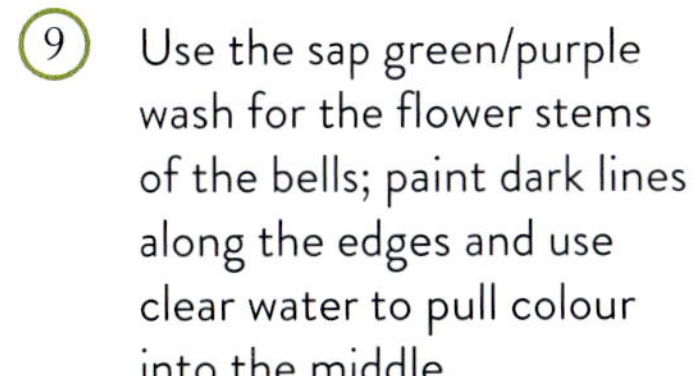

Mix a sap green/olive green wash to fill the stem.

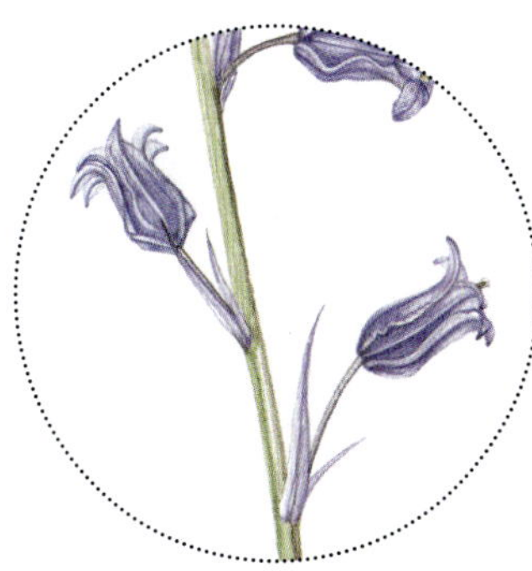

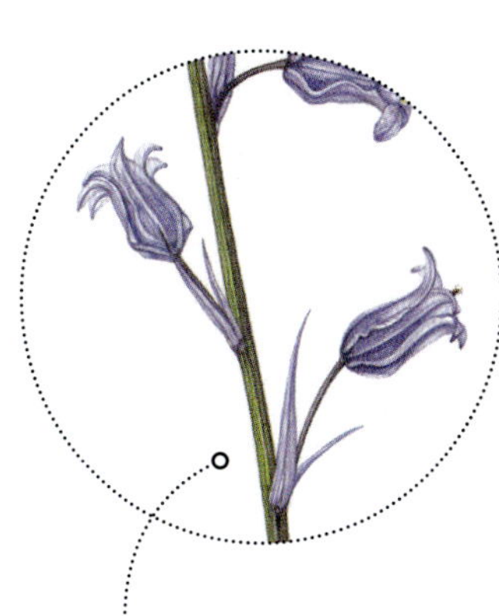

Use a lemon yellow wash for the highlight on the left-hand side of the stem.

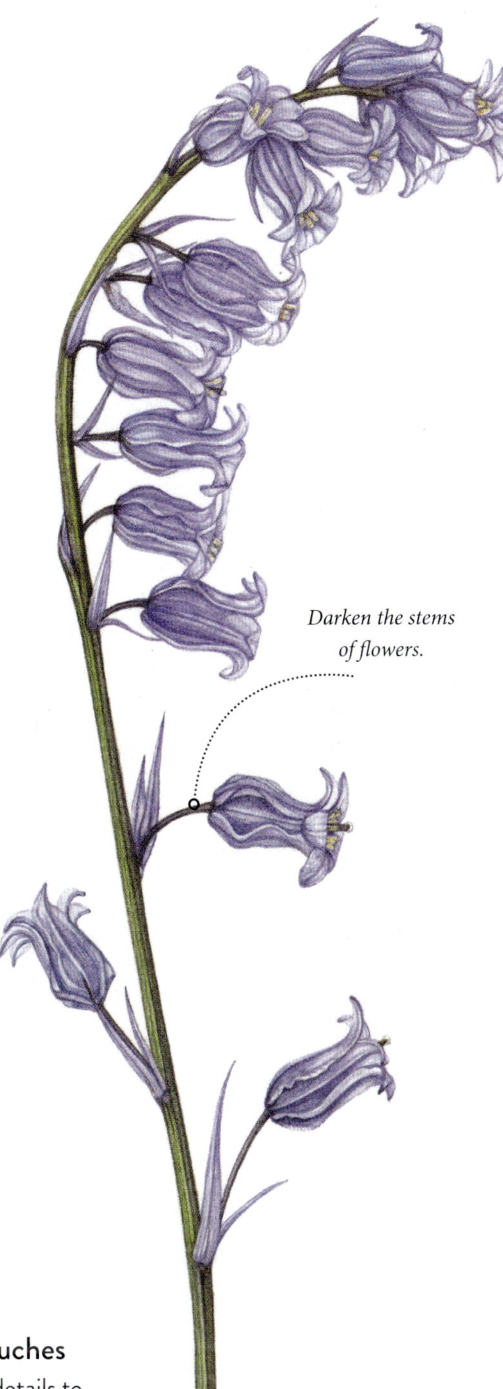

Darken the stems of flowers.

10 **Finishing touches**

Add any final details to the sepals. Add a touch of cadmium red to the stamens.

How to paint a whole plant with roots

With its head of fine petals, smooth hollow stem, strongly veined leaves and deep taproot, the humble dandelion makes the perfect subject for a whole-plant study. Unless otherwise stated, I have used a small brush throughout.

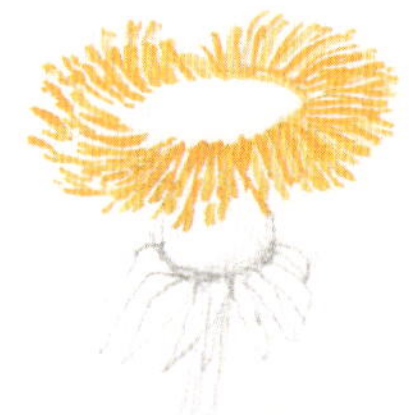
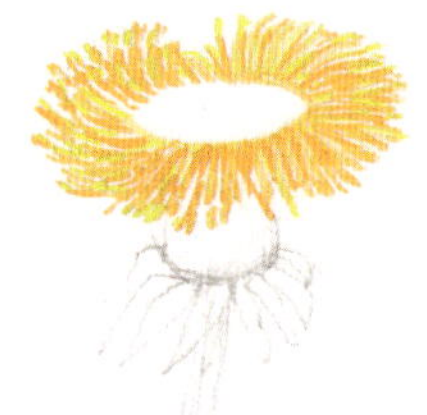
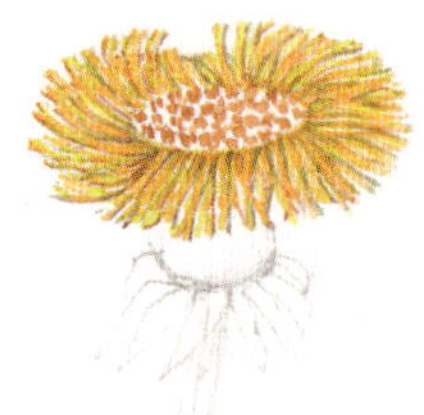

① **Start with the flower**
Mix a cadmium yellow pale wash. Paint each petal separately, leaving small white lines between them. Paint outwards from the centre of the flower and fork the ends of the petals.

② Use a lemon yellow wash to highlight brighter sections of the flower. Work in the same way as you did for step 1.

③ Mix cadmium red, burnt sienna and violet for a dark red wash. Use this to darken where the petals overlap. Paint the furled petals at the centre using a lemon yellow pale/cadmium red mix. Outline some of the petals with a sap green wash.

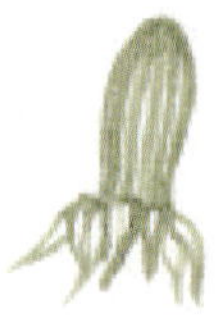
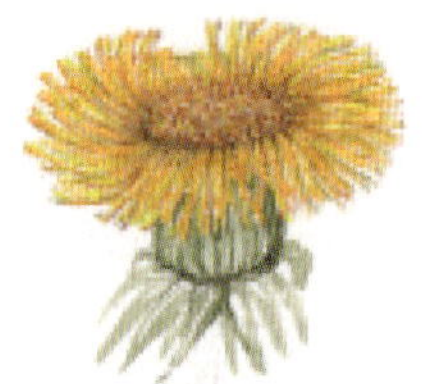
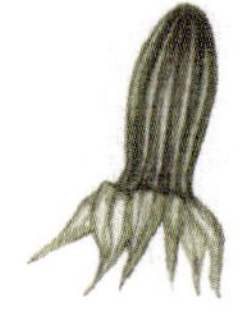
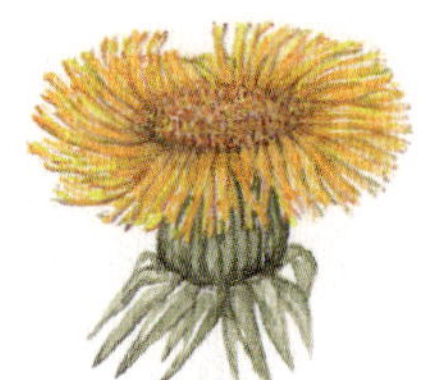
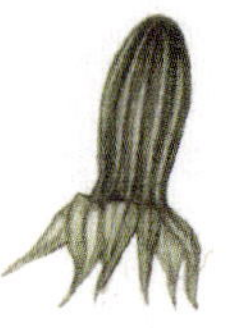
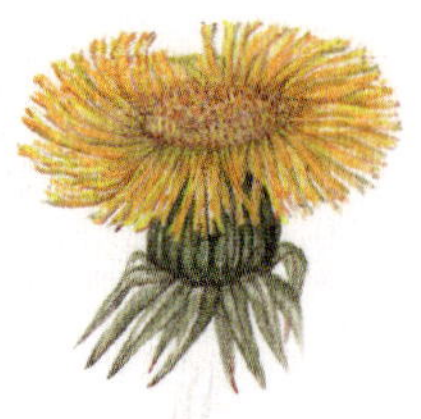

④ **Include the bud**
Fill the centre of the flower using a lemon yellow wash, then add a little texture using the darker wash from step 3. Apply a sap green wash to the base of the flower, its bracts and the bud. Paint flowing strokes that follow their form.

⑤ Use a violet/sap green wash to add shadows and darker areas to the base of the flower, its bracts and the bud. Follow their form.

⑥ Using a very small brush, apply strokes of cadmium red to the tips and veins of the bracts. Use the same wash to refine the bulbous form at the base of the flower.

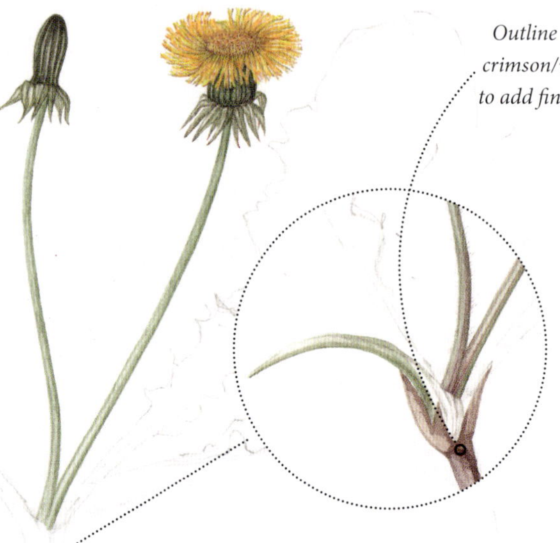

Outline the stem with cadmium red. Mix an alizarin crimson/violet wash to fill the stem. Use the same wash to add fine lines at the base of the bud and flower stems.

⑦ **Paint the stems and roots**
Apply a watery wash of sap green to the stems. Follow this with a darker wash of the same colour, applying it just to the sides of the stems.

⑧ To paint the lower bract, apply a sap green wash to the outer edge and use water to pull colour into the rest of the bract. Using a Payne's grey wash, add fine lines to show the bract's veins and creases.

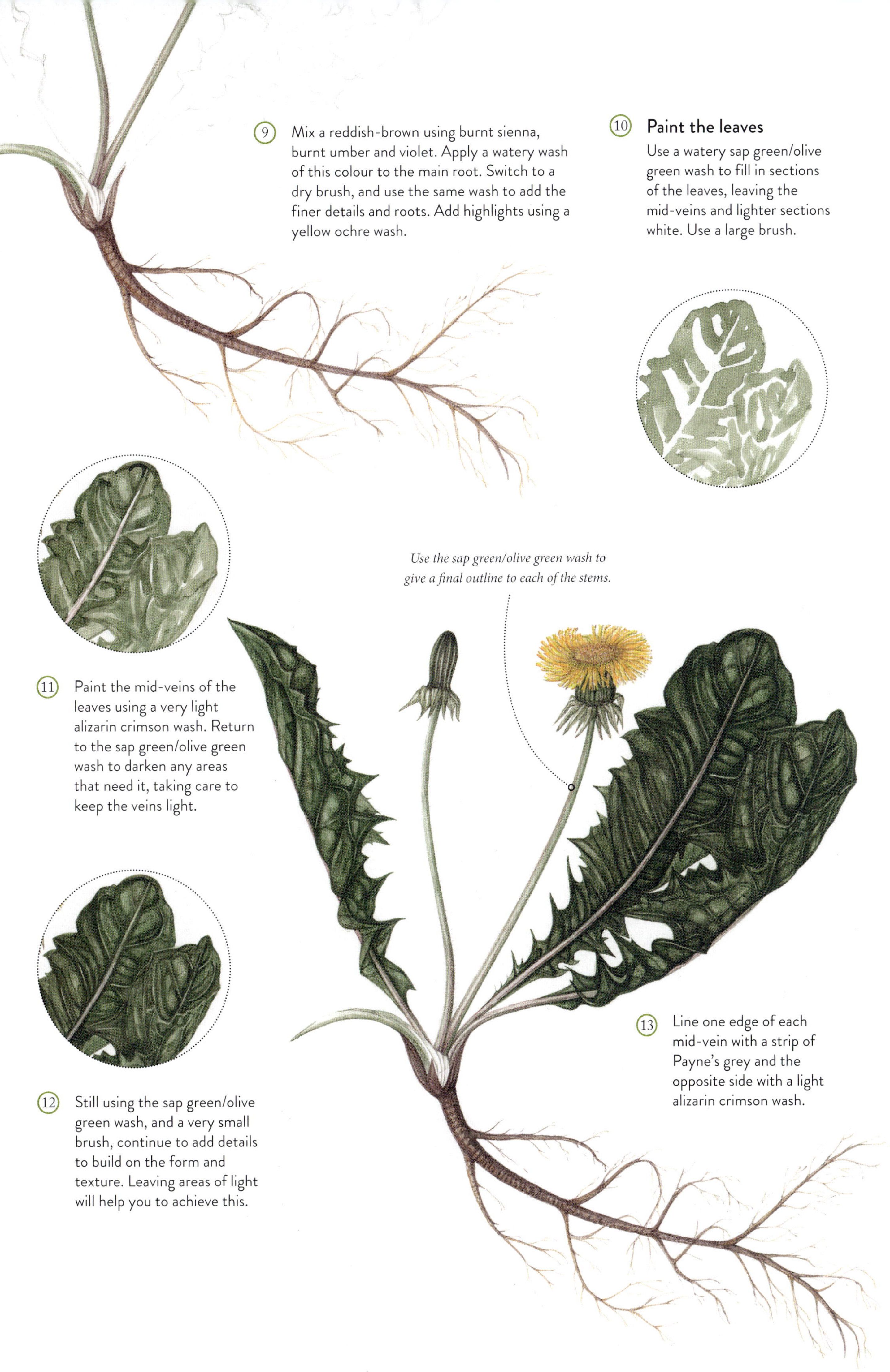

9. Mix a reddish-brown using burnt sienna, burnt umber and violet. Apply a watery wash of this colour to the main root. Switch to a dry brush, and use the same wash to add the finer details and roots. Add highlights using a yellow ochre wash.

10. **Paint the leaves**
Use a watery sap green/olive green wash to fill in sections of the leaves, leaving the mid-veins and lighter sections white. Use a large brush.

Use the sap green/olive green wash to give a final outline to each of the stems.

11. Paint the mid-veins of the leaves using a very light alizarin crimson wash. Return to the sap green/olive green wash to darken any areas that need it, taking care to keep the veins light.

12. Still using the sap green/olive green wash, and a very small brush, continue to add details to build on the form and texture. Leaving areas of light will help you to achieve this.

13. Line one edge of each mid-vein with a strip of Payne's grey and the opposite side with a light alizarin crimson wash.

How to paint surface details

Cuckoo pint is a woodland flowering plant in which the flowers are hidden just above where the stem starts. What is visible is the upper portion of the spadix protected by a large bract. I chose this wildflower for its iconic, sculptural shape and beautiful leaves. The tutorial focuses on adding small surface details on the spathe and creating the dark, shiny leaf.

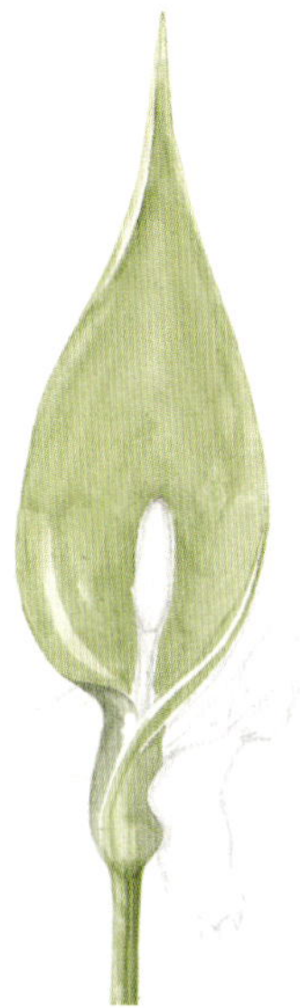

1. **Start with the bract**
Use a sap green, olive green and lemon yellow wash to apply block colour to the bract and stem. Use a large brush and leave white highlights where the bract curls at the edges. Keep the spadix white.

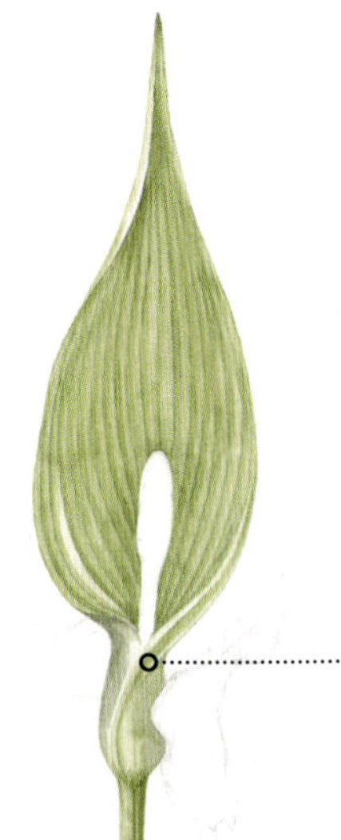

2. Use a watery sap green wash and a small paintbrush to mark veins on the bract. Keep your lines roughly the same distance apart. Shade behind the veins with a watery wash of sap green, to show the veins are ridged.

Apply another wash of sap green where the bract folds around the spadix, painting right up to the spadix.

3. Using a thicker sap green wash, paint horizontal lines between the veins, using a small paintbrush with a fine point. Paint the vertical veins on the bump above the stem, curving them slightly to capture its form.

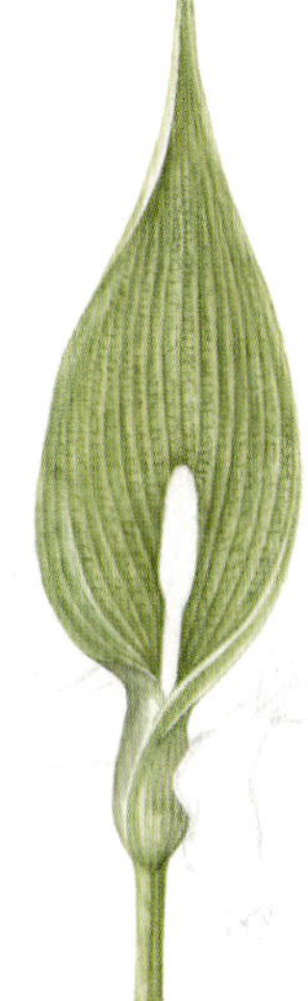

4. Use a large brush to apply a wash of lemon yellow over the bract and stem to brighten. Use clean water and a large brush to soften the edges of the veins and to lift patches of colour on the bract.

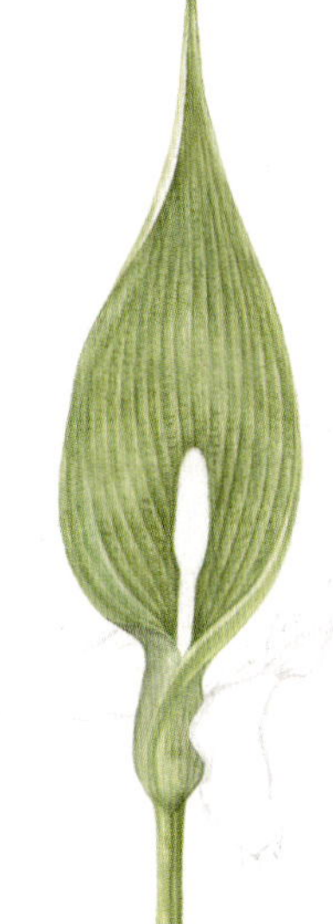

5. Use the step 3 wash to darken the right-hand side of each vein, creating a highlight on the curve of each ridge. Use the same wash to define the rolled section at the top of the bract. Where the bract wraps around the stem, apply a light violet/sap green mix to the side catching the light and darken the mix for the side in shadow. Paint the spadix using a very dark violet, alizarin crimson and Payne's grey mix.

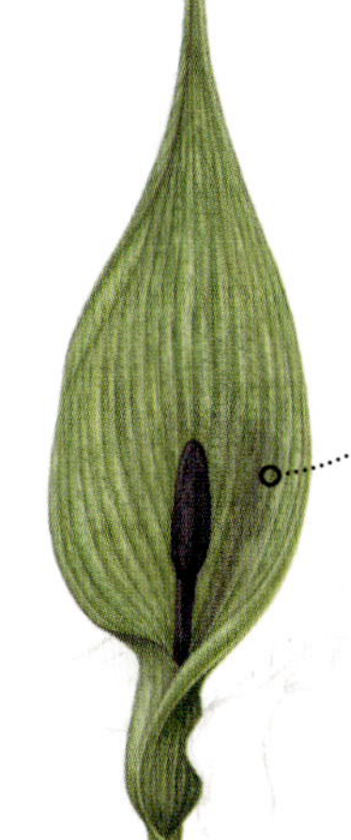

Use the darker violet/sap green mix to add more texture in shaded areas.

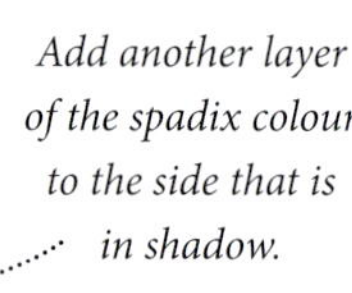

Add another layer of the spadix colour to the side that is in shadow.

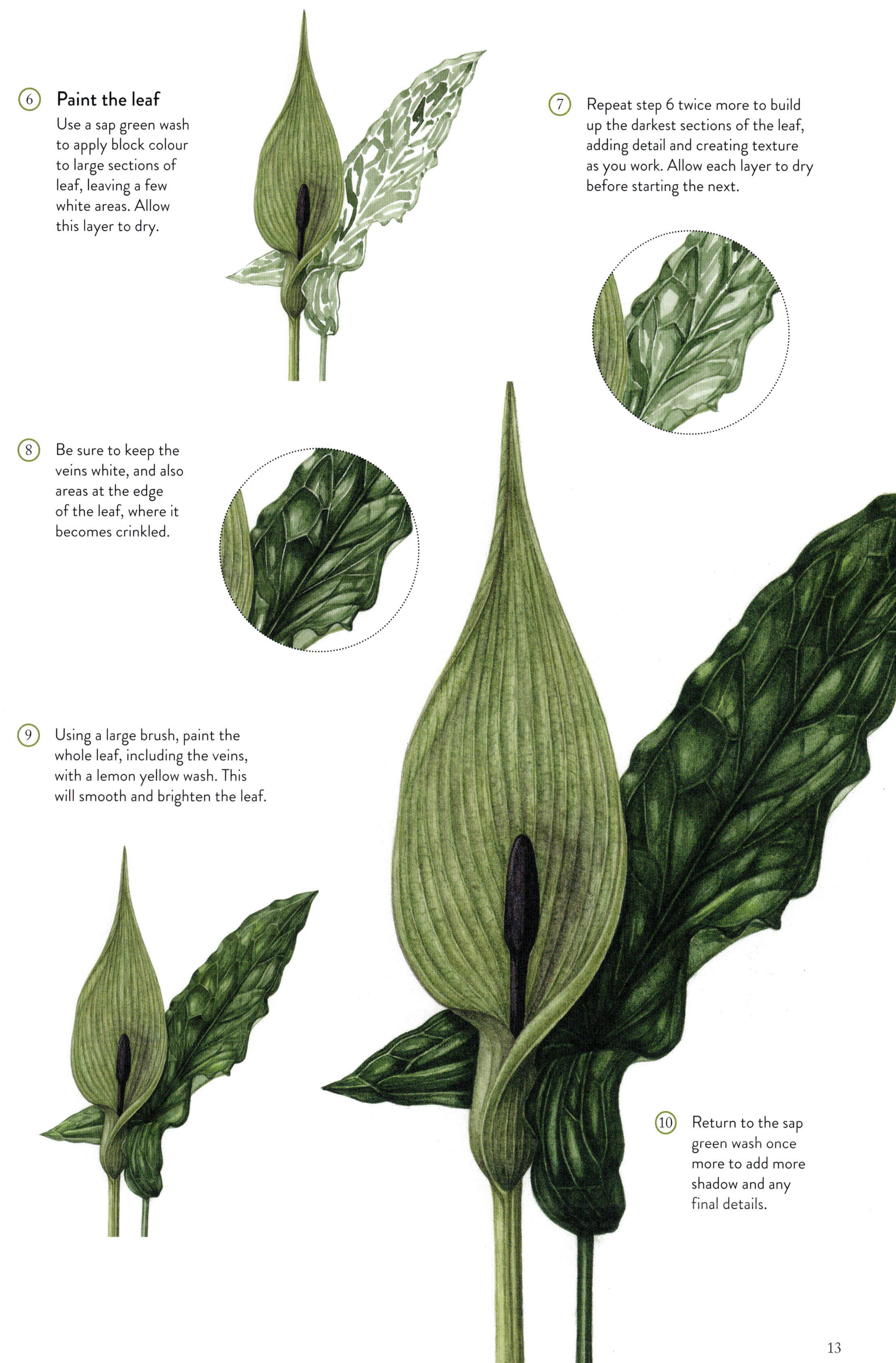

(6) **Paint the leaf**
Use a sap green wash to apply block colour to large sections of leaf, leaving a few white areas. Allow this layer to dry.

(7) Repeat step 6 twice more to build up the darkest sections of the leaf, adding detail and creating texture as you work. Allow each layer to dry before starting the next.

(8) Be sure to keep the veins white, and also areas at the edge of the leaf, where it becomes crinkled.

(9) Using a large brush, paint the whole leaf, including the veins, with a lemon yellow wash. This will smooth and brighten the leaf.

(10) Return to the sap green wash once more to add more shadow and any final details.

How to paint complex compositions

I have chosen a ball of crab apple blossom and leaves for this tutorial. There is very little space between the elements and one leaf overlaps another. This is a great opportunity to look very carefully at cast shadows and use the green of the leaves to highlight the edges of the petals, making them appear bright white.

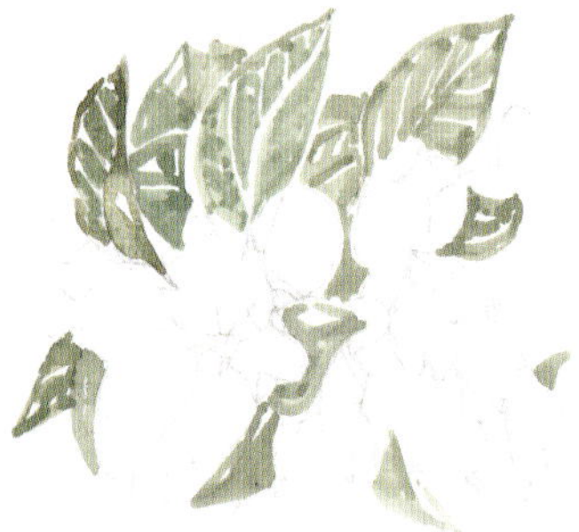

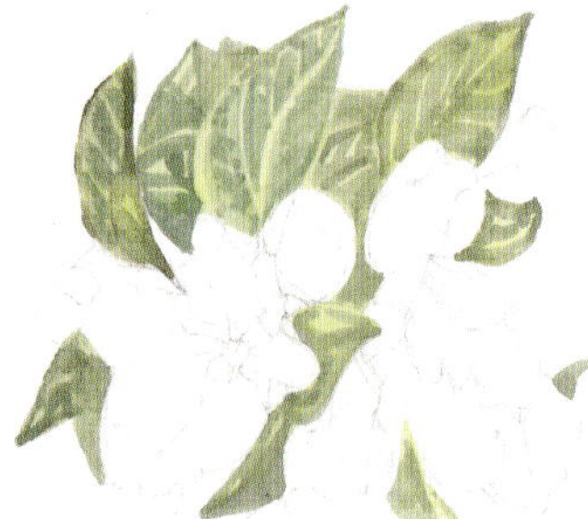

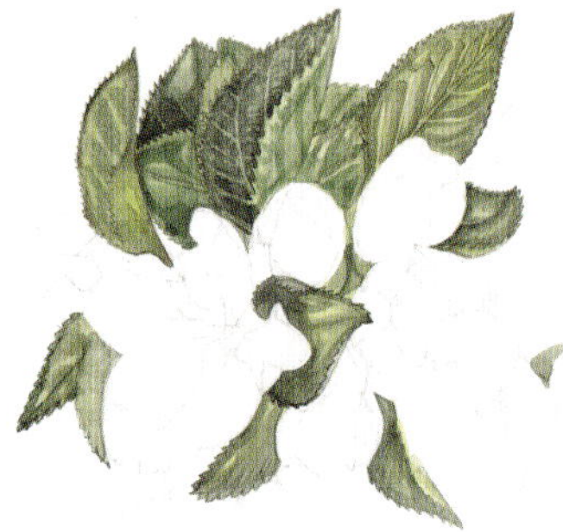

① **Start with the leaves**
Make a sap green/olive green wash and block in the green of the leaves using a large brush. Leave white spaces for the veins and lighter areas of the leaves.

② Still using a large brush, apply a thin lemon yellow wash over all of the leaves.

③ Return to the sap green/olive green wash and use a small brush to paint into the teeth at the leaf edges. Use the same colour to pick out the veins, the shadows behind the veins and shadows cast by the leaves.

④ Repeat steps 2 and 3 to add depth and detail to the leaves, taking care not to paint over the veins. Add violet to the green mix and use this to define the darkest areas. Allow the paint to dry.

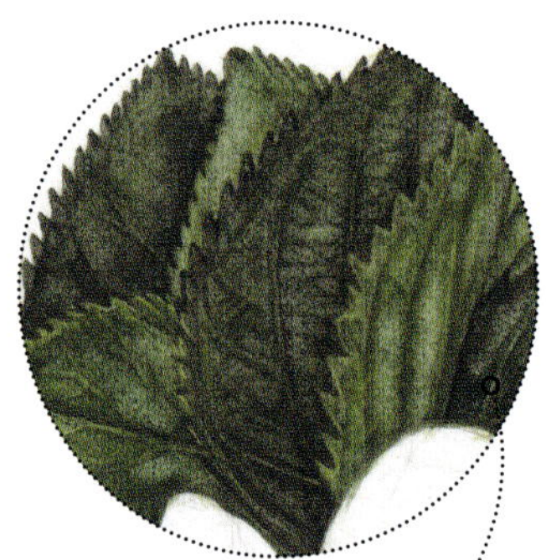

Reapply the green/ violet wash to the darkest areas.

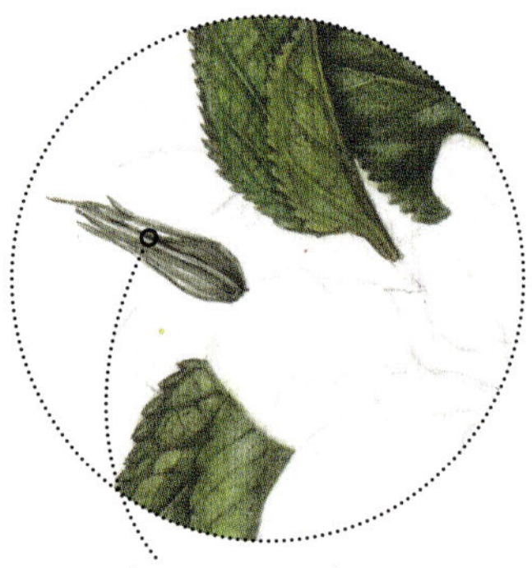

Use the sap green/olive green to paint the flower bud and the green/violet to add darker lines to give it form and detail.

⑤ **Paint the petals**
Make a light wash of permanent rose, permanent alizarin crimson and opera rose. Using a clean brush, apply clear water to the areas of the petals that will be pink. Gently add the colour and watch it flow into the clean water. Add more colour to the darker pink areas so that you start to show the structure of the petal.

⑥ Use a very light Payne's grey wash to add shadows and creases in the petals. Take care not to overdo it; the aim is for the petals to stay looking white with shadows.

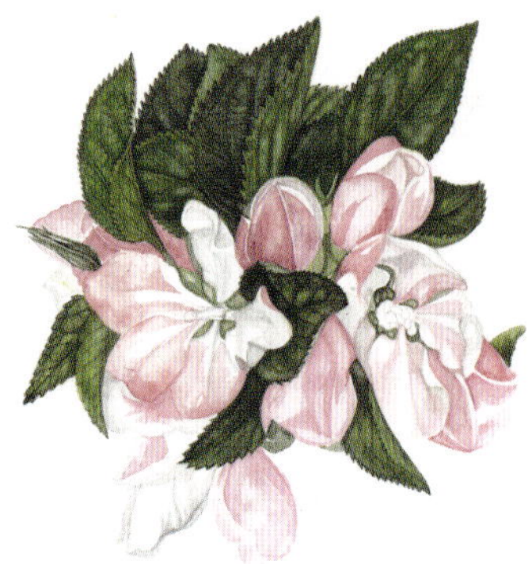

7. Use the pink wash to darken areas of the petals that are in shadow. Switch to a very fine brush to paint in the veins and creases of the petals; follow the form so the structure of the petals is not flattened. Add a few lines and details with the Payne's grey.

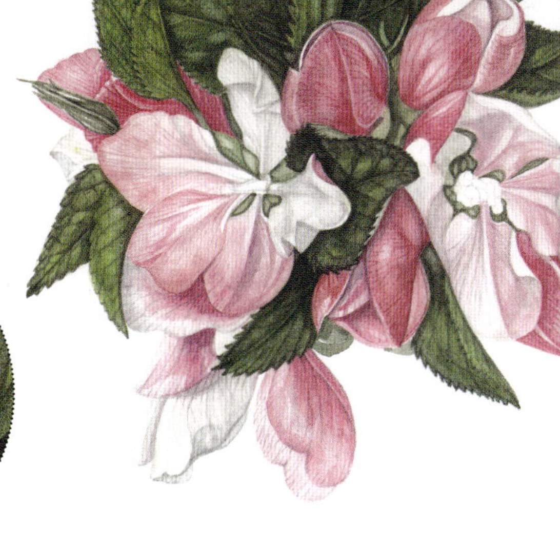

8. **Finishing touches**
Remove a little colour from the leaves to help capture their form. Apply clear water to a section, allow it to sink in and then lift off some colour using a clean tissue.

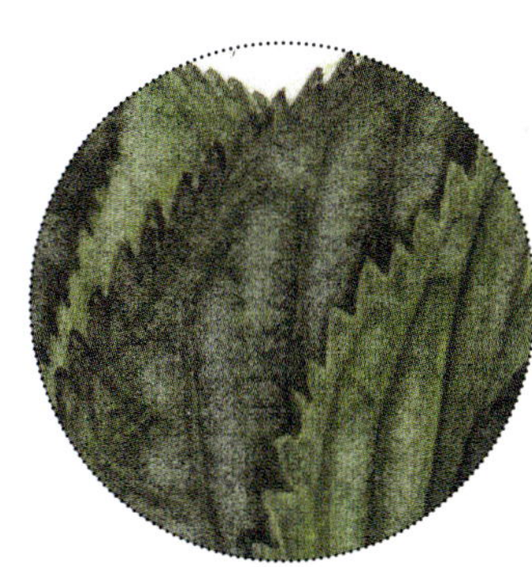

9. Use the pink and grey washes to further darken any areas that need it on the petals.

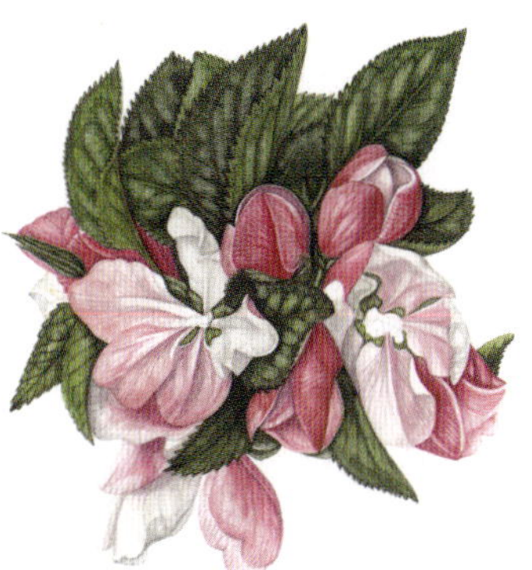

10. Use a very light sap green to paint the filaments and styles of the flowers. The anthers are three different colours, depending on the age of the pollen: pale lemon yellow; cadmium yellow; and Indian red. Block these in with light washes.

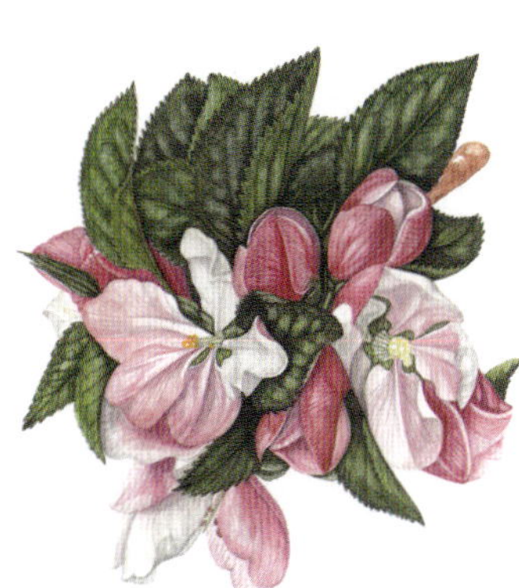

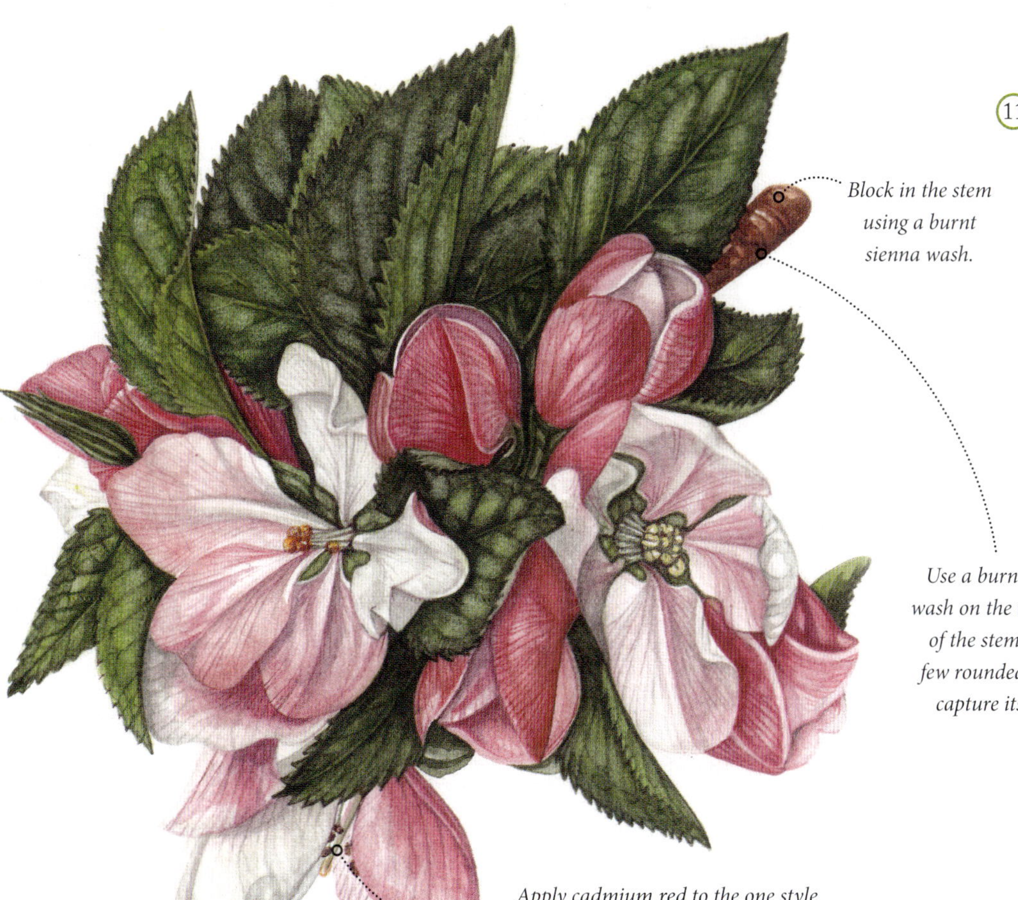

11. Use darker versions of the cadmium yellow and Indian red washes to add shadows to their respective anthers. On the palest anthers, use a wash of Payne's grey to show structure. Use the same grey between the anthers to show shadow and outline.

GALLERY

Left
CUCKOO PINT
Arum maculatum

02   09
10   13
14   15

Right
BEE ORCHID
Ophrys apifera

02   04
08   09
10   14
15

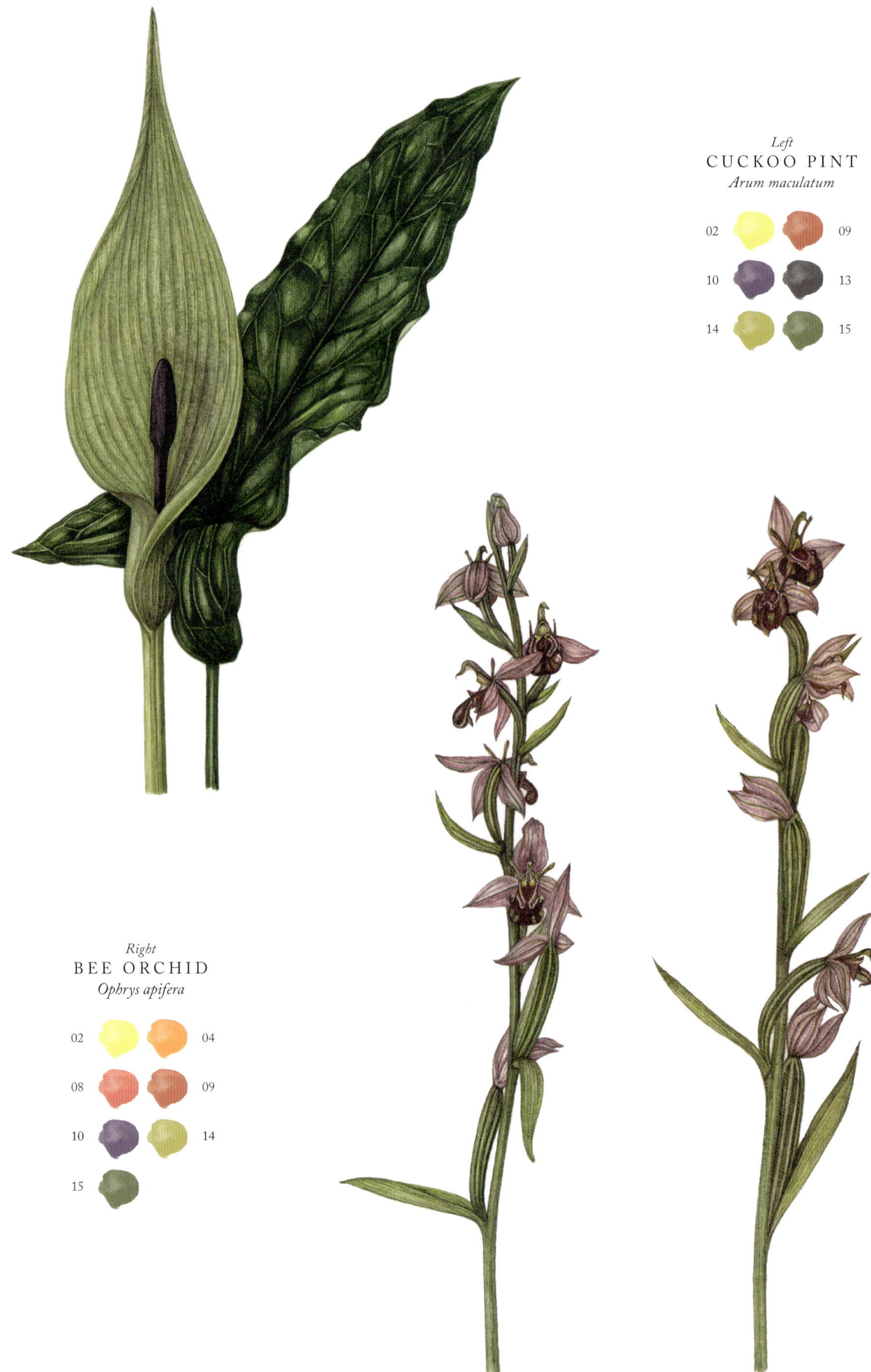

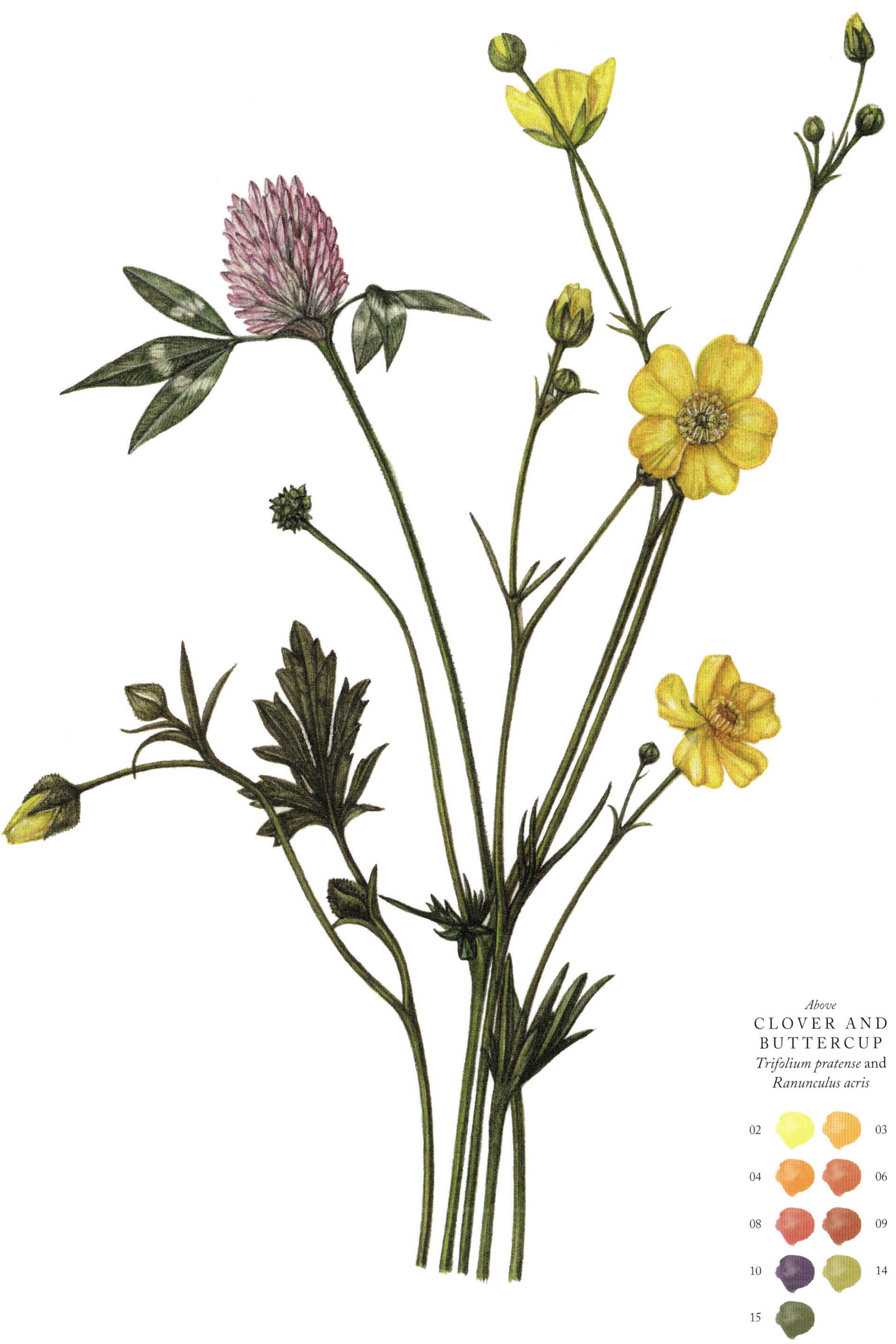

Above
CLOVER AND
BUTTERCUP
Trifolium pratense and
Ranunculus acris

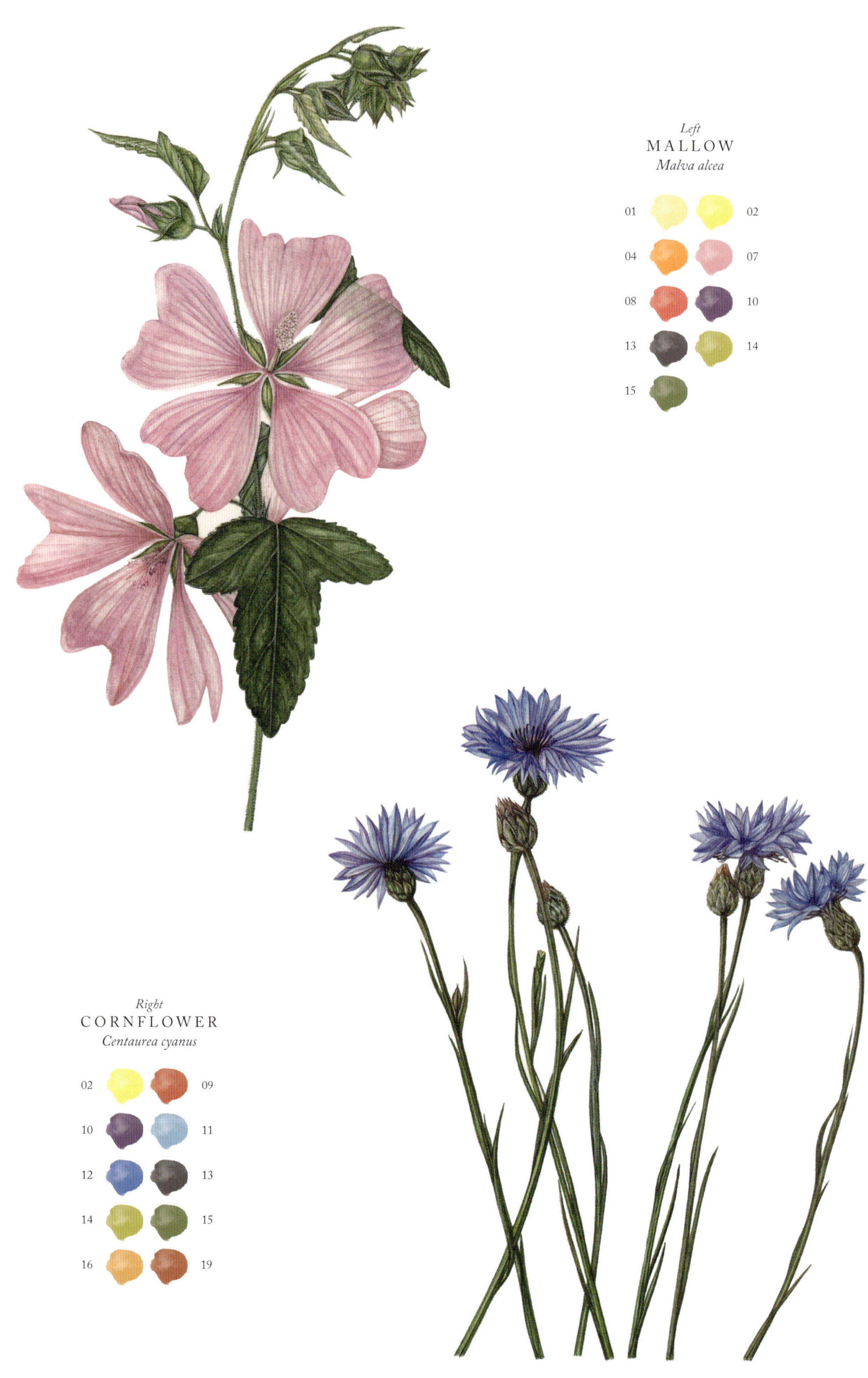

Left
MALLOW
Malva alcea

01   02
04   07
08   10
13   14
15

Right
CORNFLOWER
Centaurea cyanus

02   09
10   11
12   13
14   15
16   19

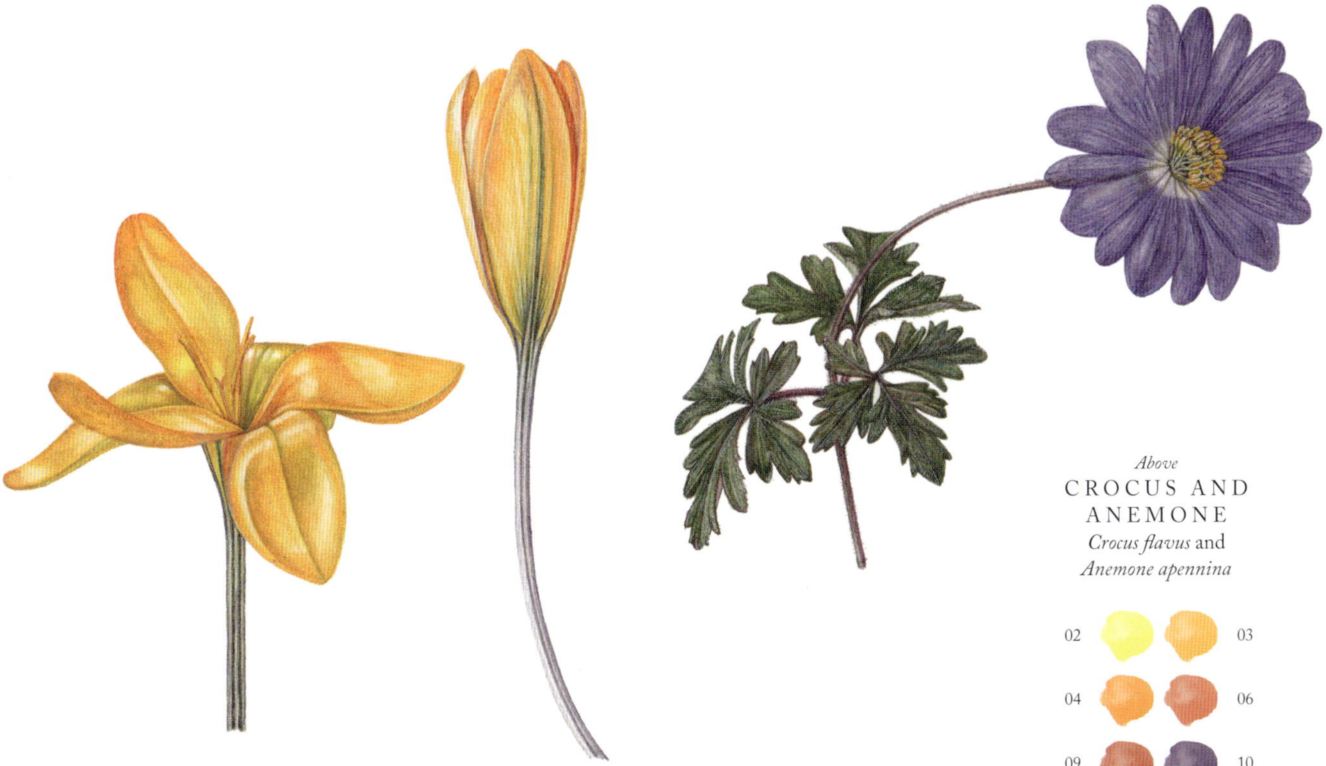

CROCUS AND ANEMONE
Crocus flavus and
Anemone apennina

02 03
04 06
09 10
11 13
14 15
16 19

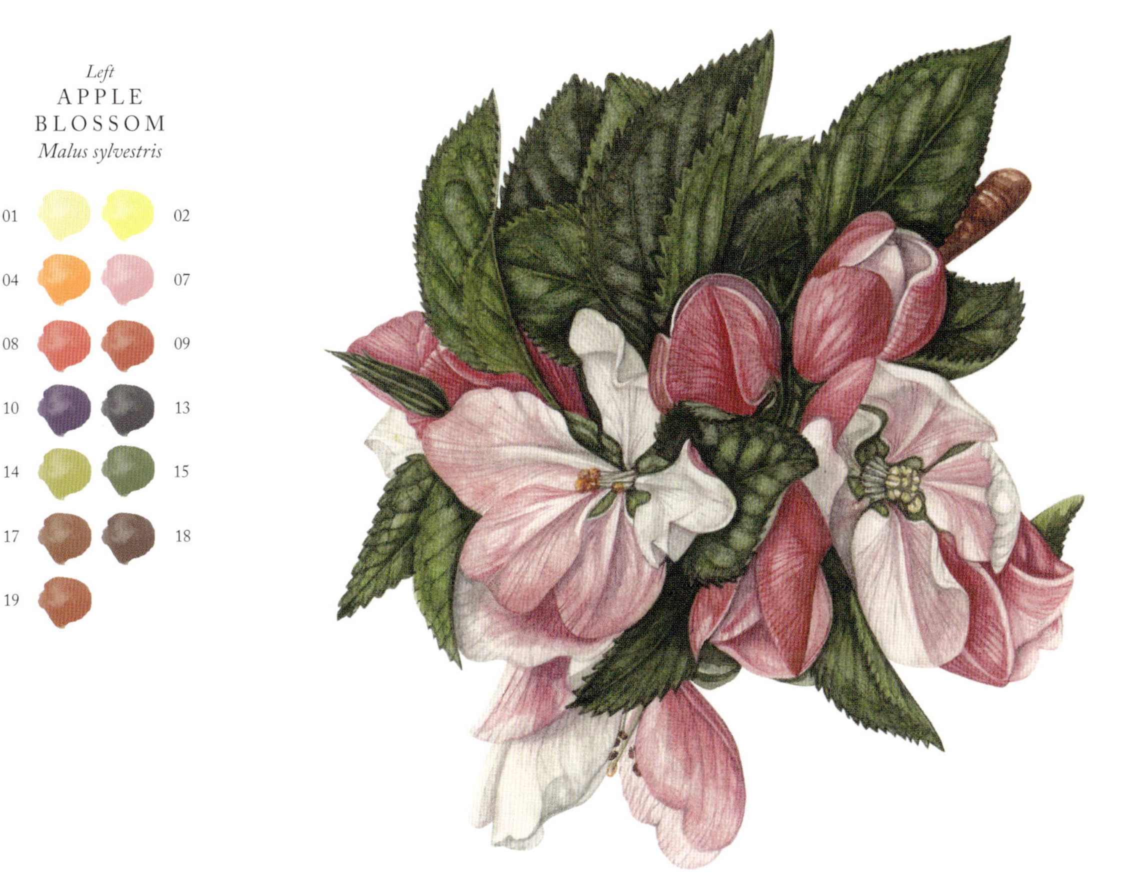

APPLE BLOSSOM
Malus sylvestris

01 02
04 07
08 09
10 13
14 15
17 18
19

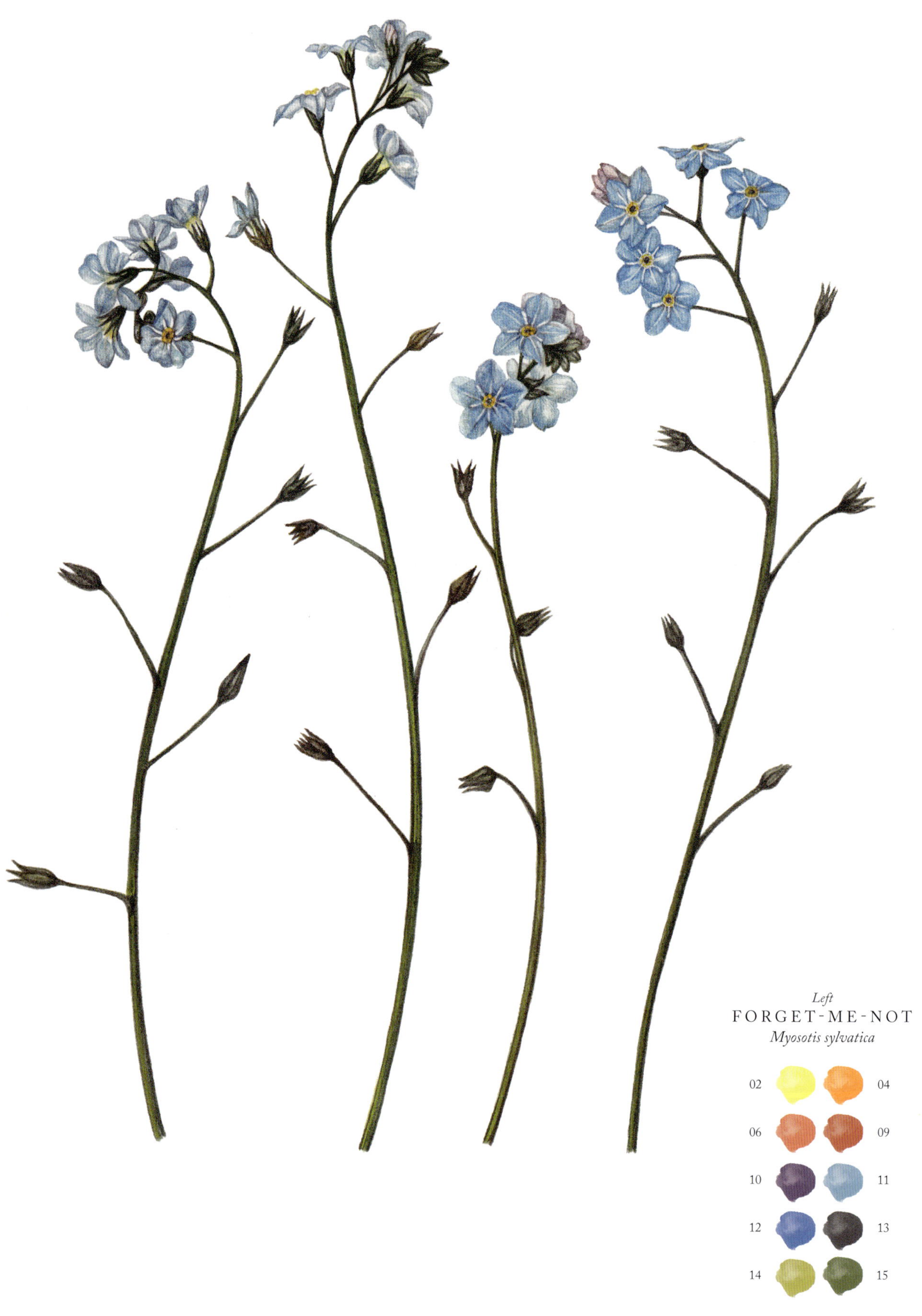

Left
FORGET-ME-NOT
Myosotis sylvatica

02
04
06
09
10
11
12
13
14
15

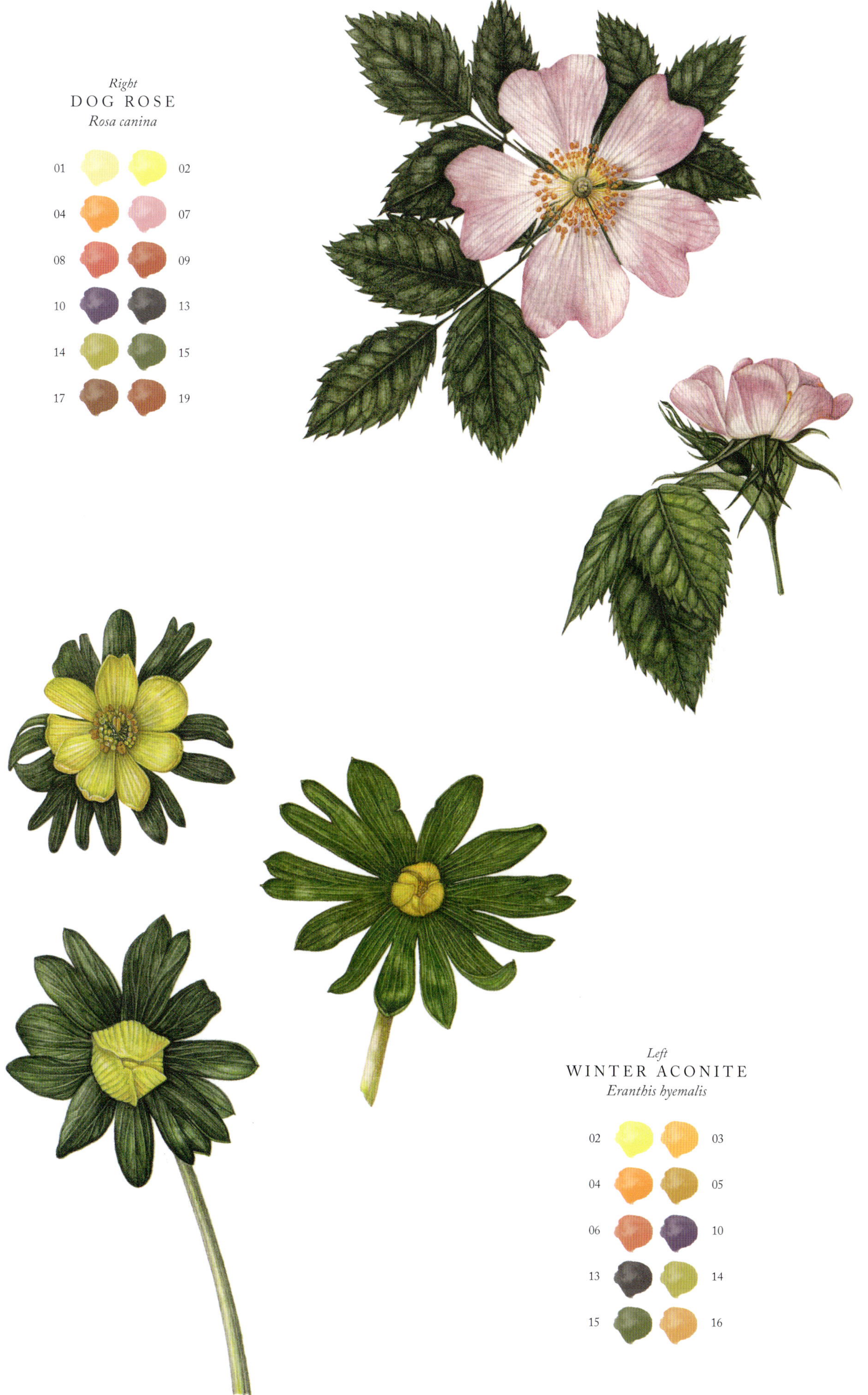
Right
DOG ROSE
Rosa canina

01
02
04
07
08
09
10
13
14
15
17
19

Left
WINTER ACONITE
Eranthis hyemalis

02
03
04
05
06
10
13
14
15
16

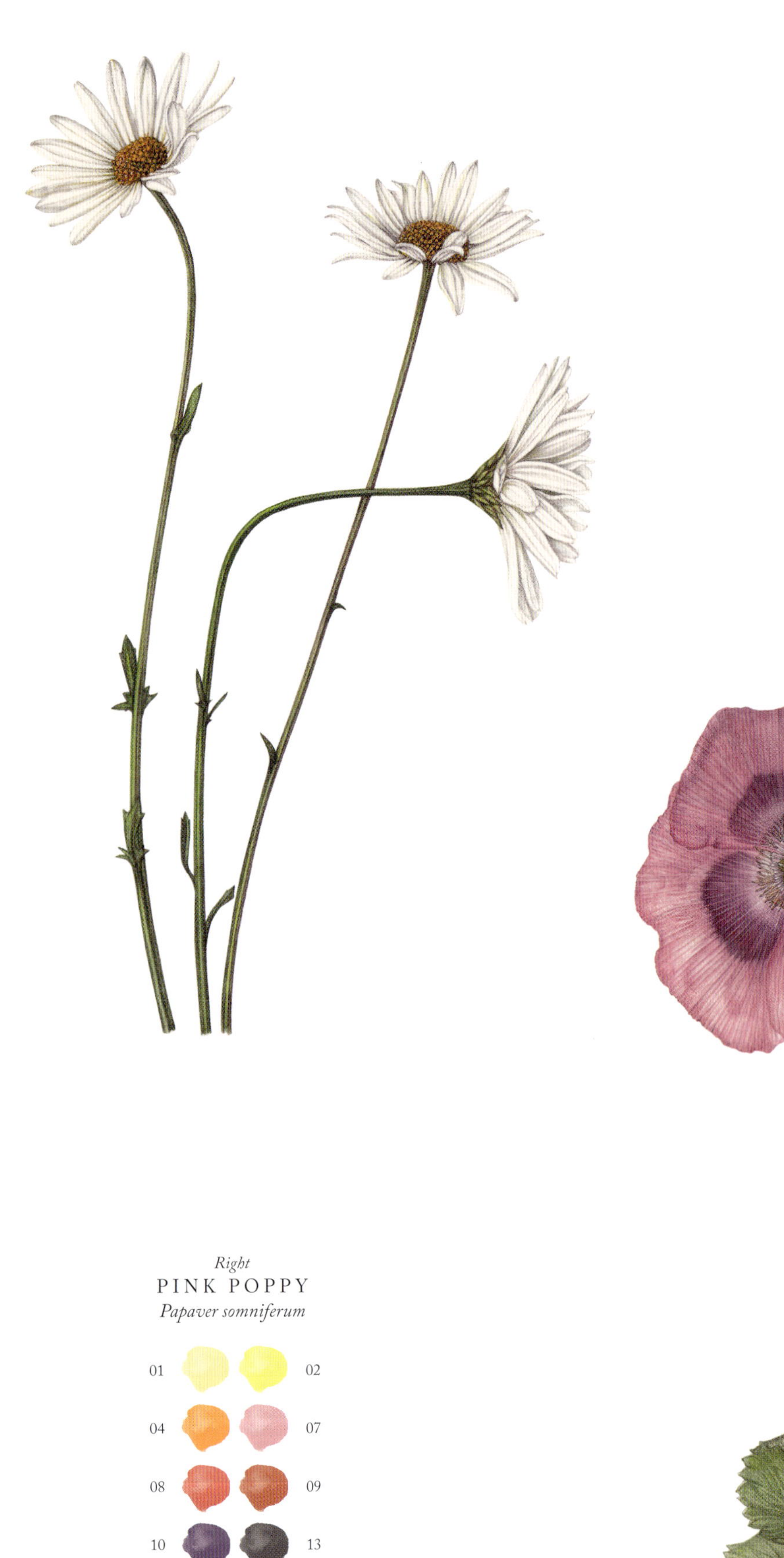

Left
OX-EYE DAISY
Leucanthemum vulgare

02   04
06   10
13   14
15   19

Right
PINK POPPY
Papaver somniferum

01   02
04   07
08   09
10   13
14   15

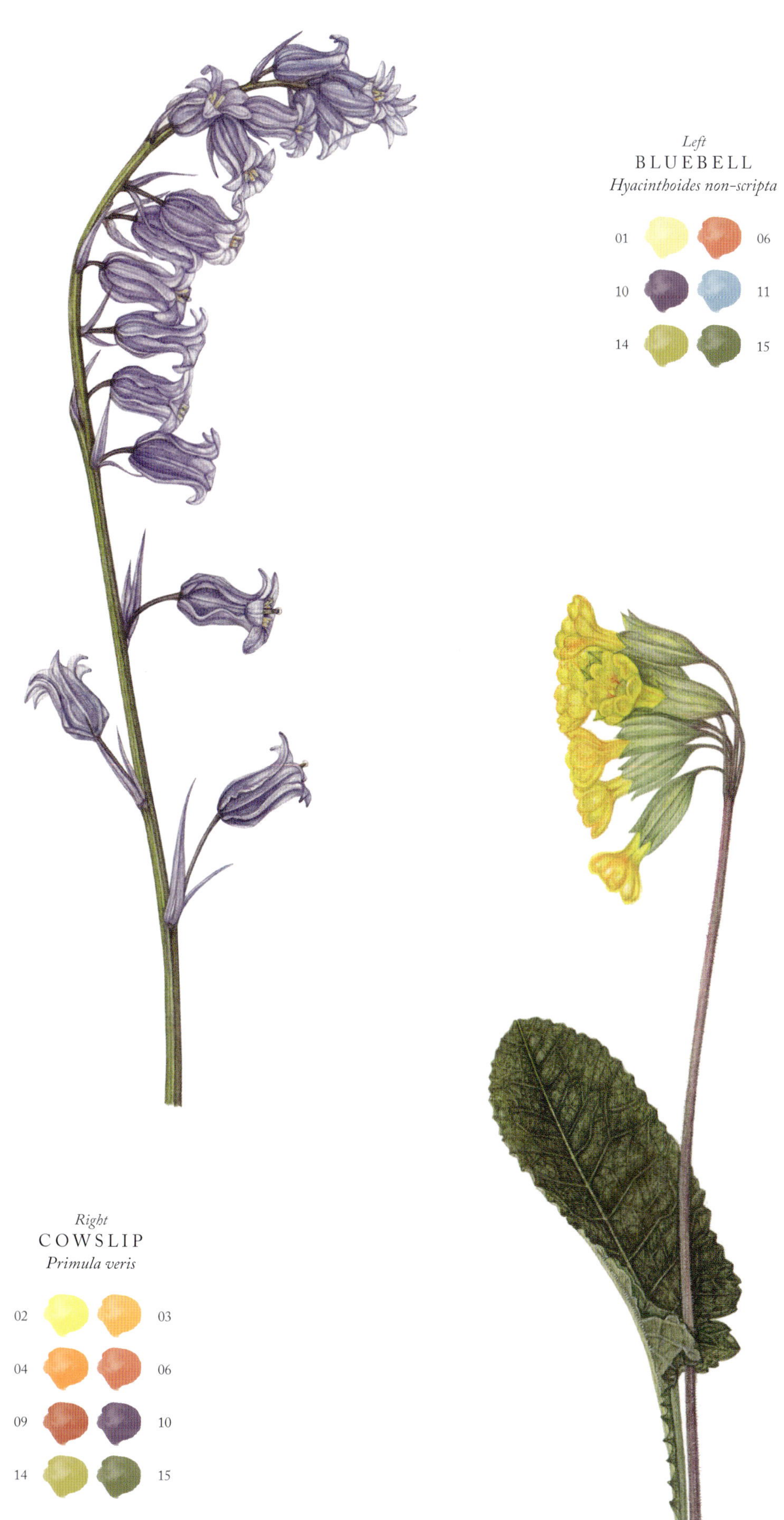

Left
BLUEBELL
Hyacinthoides non-scripta

01   06
10   11
14   15

Right
COWSLIP
Primula veris

02   03
04   06
09   10
14   15

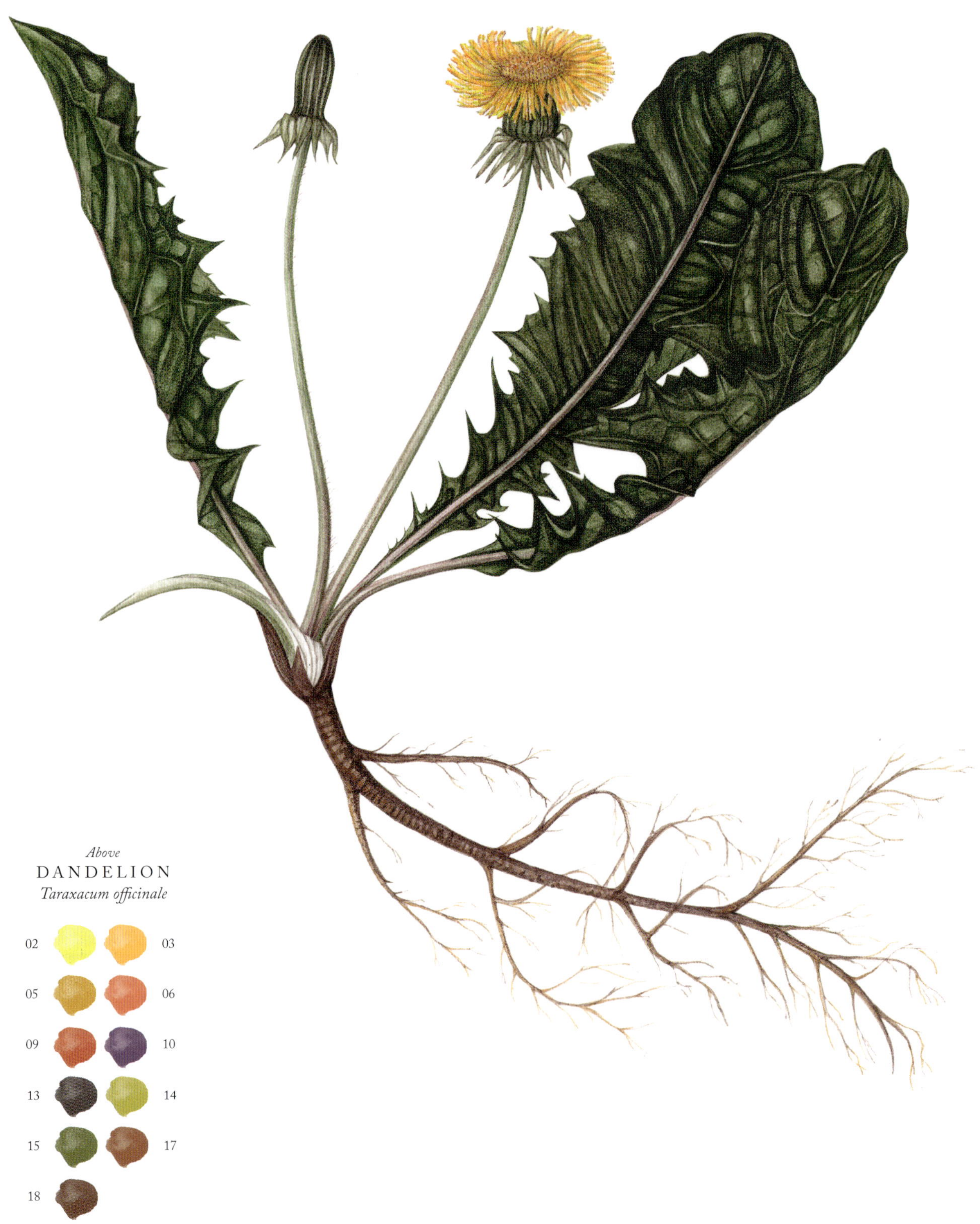

Above
DANDELION
Taraxacum officinale

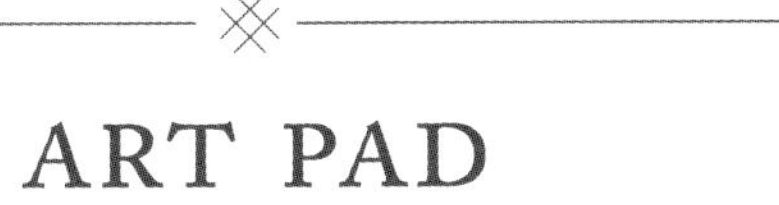

ART PAD

This section contains all the outlines you need
to complete the paintings in the gallery.

CUCKOO PINT

Arum maculatum

BEE ORCHID
Ophrys apifera

CLOVER AND BUTTERCUP
Trifolium pratense and Ranunculus acris

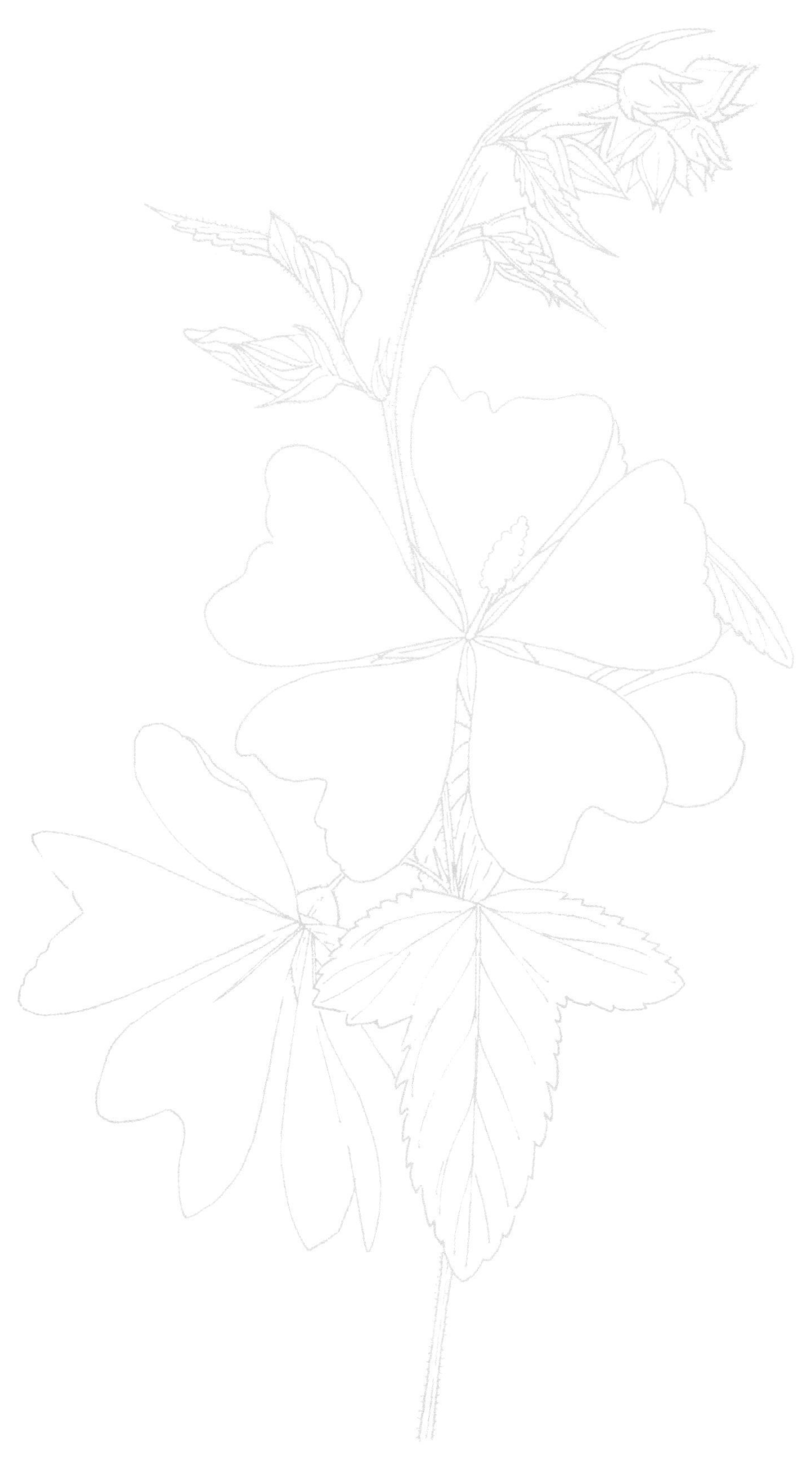

MALLOW

Malva alcea

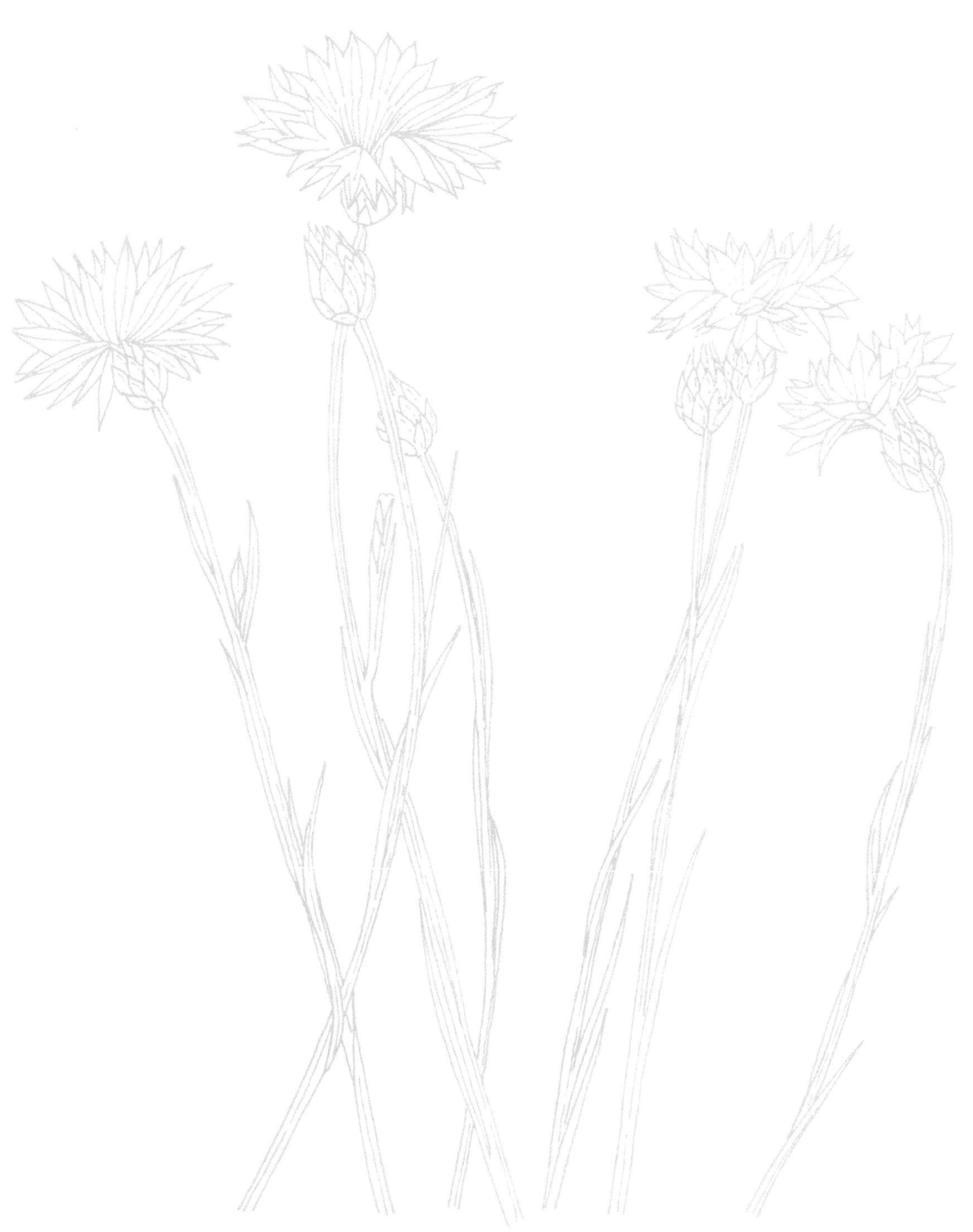

CORNFLOWER
Centaurea cyanus

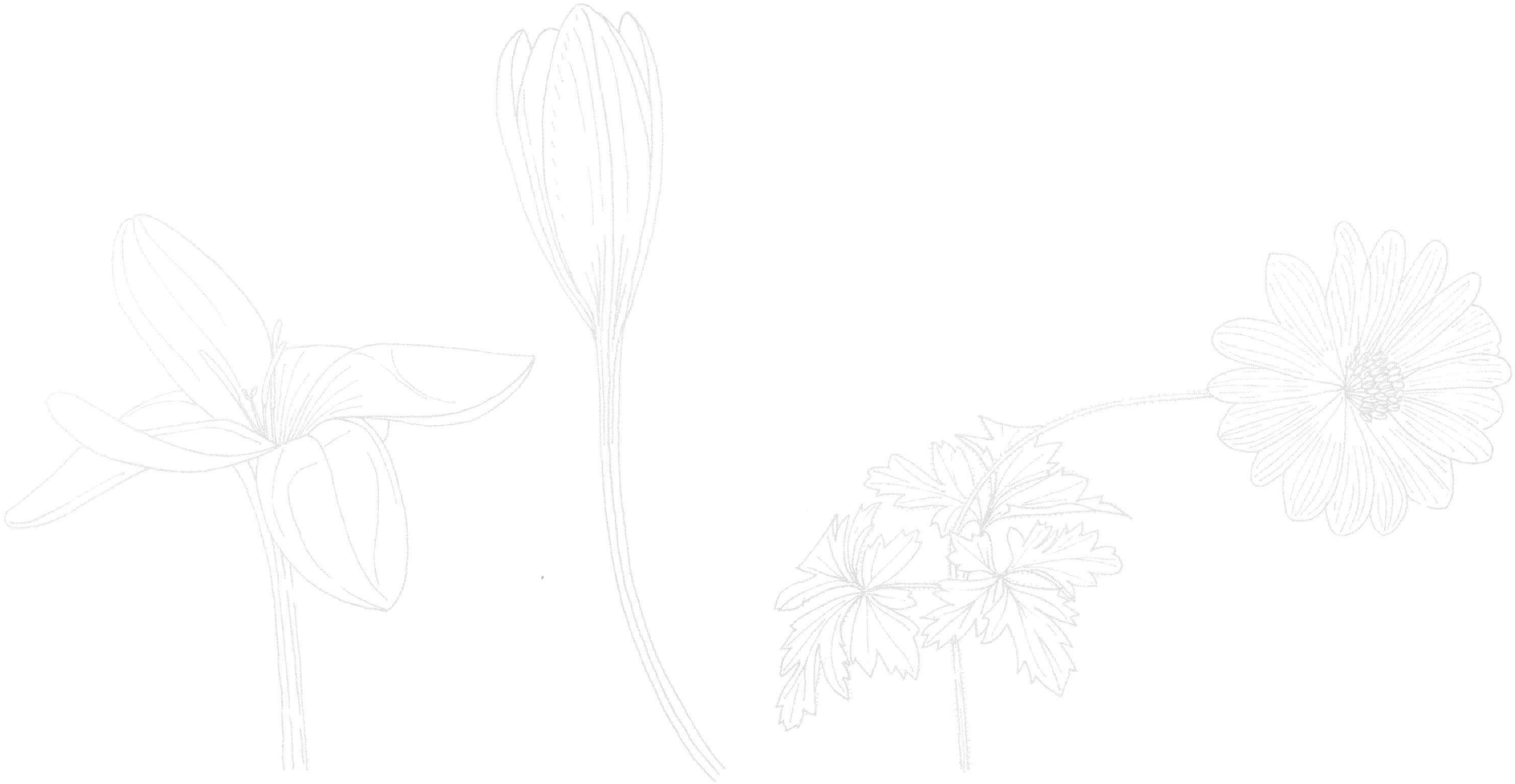

CROCUS AND ANEMONE

Crocus flavus and Anemone apennina

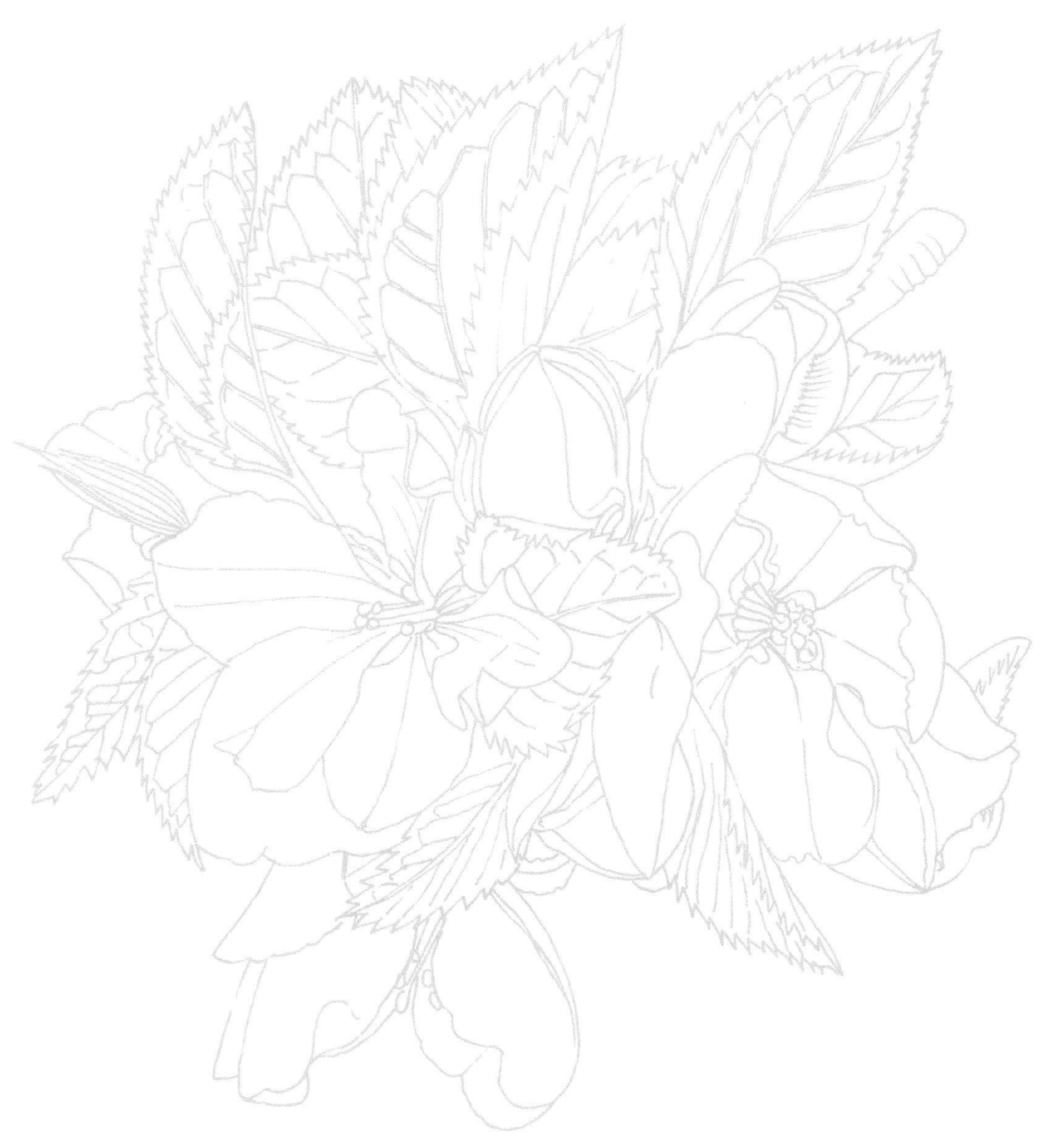

APPLE BLOSSOM

Malus sylvestris

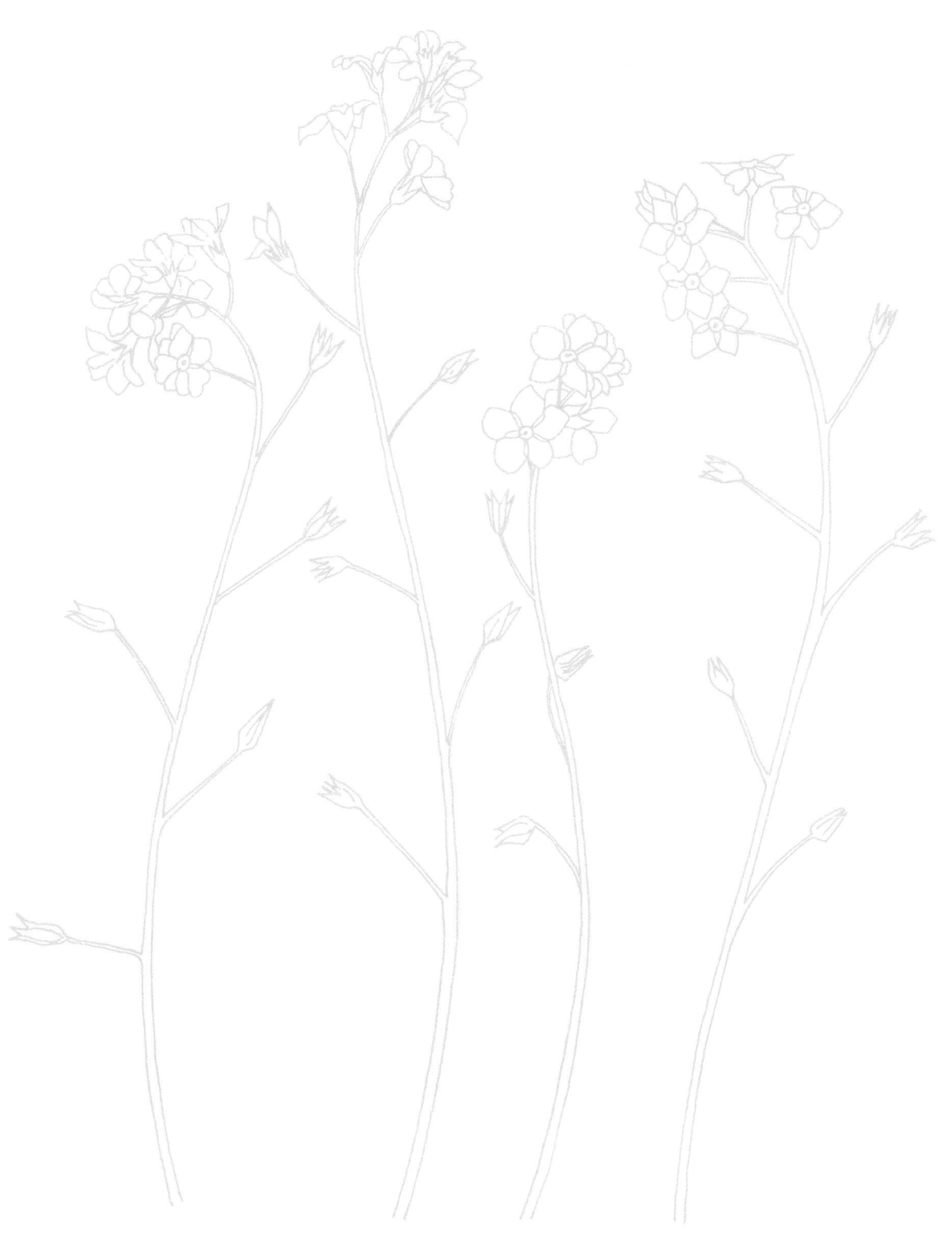

FORGET-ME-NOT
Myosotis sylvatica

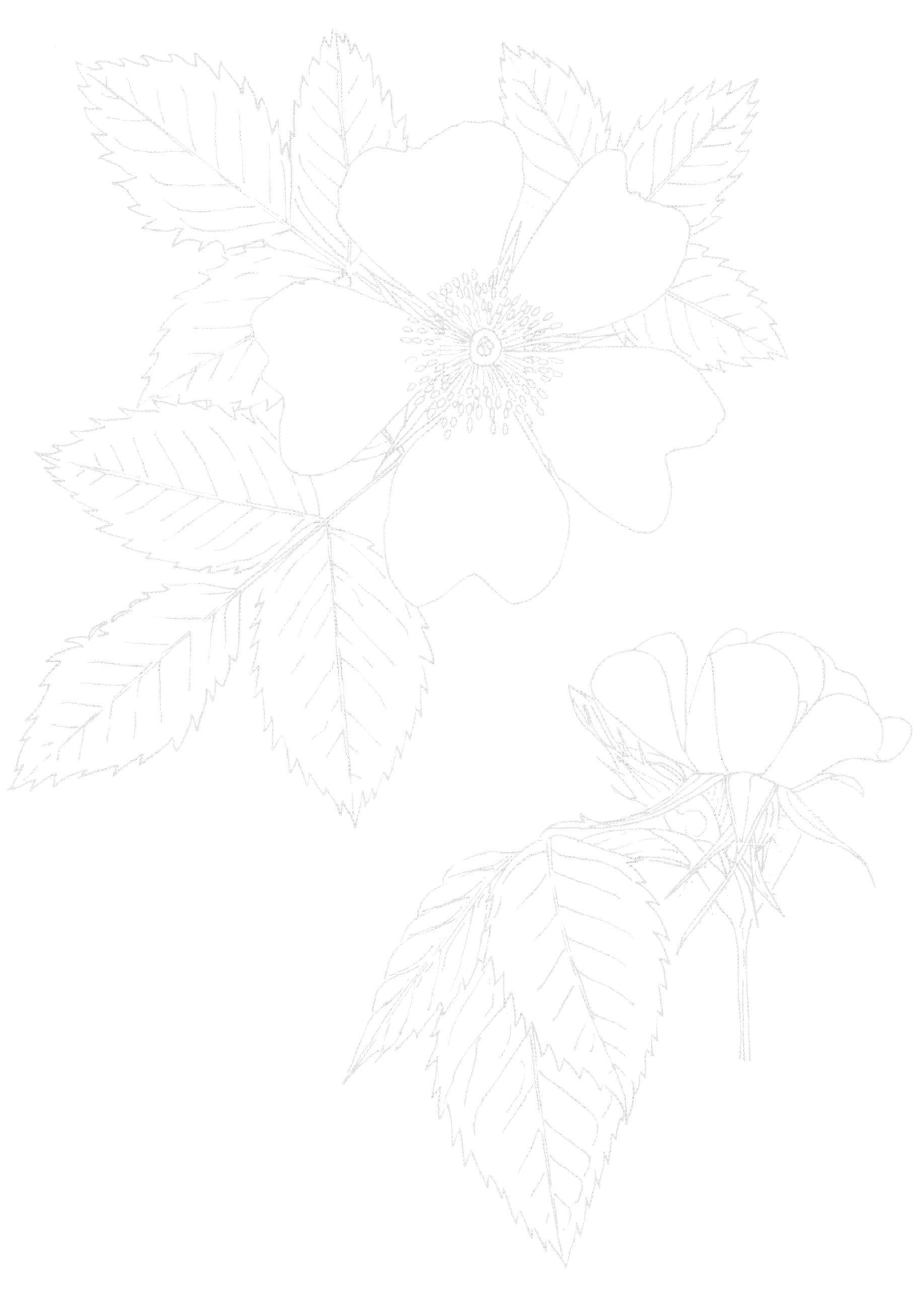

DOG ROSE

Rosa canina

WINTER ACONITE

Eranthis hyemalis

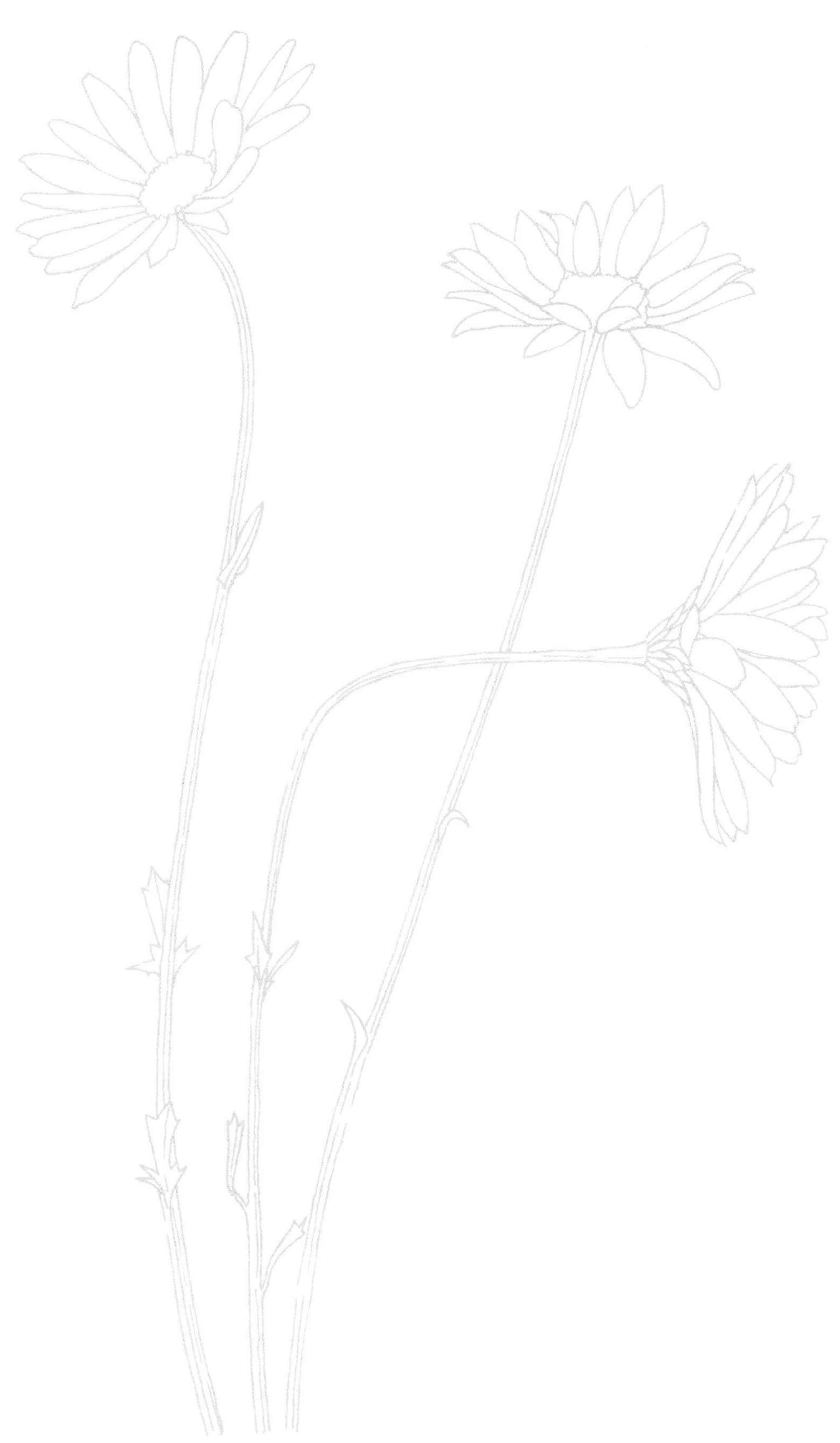

OX-EYE DAISY

Leucanthemum vulgare

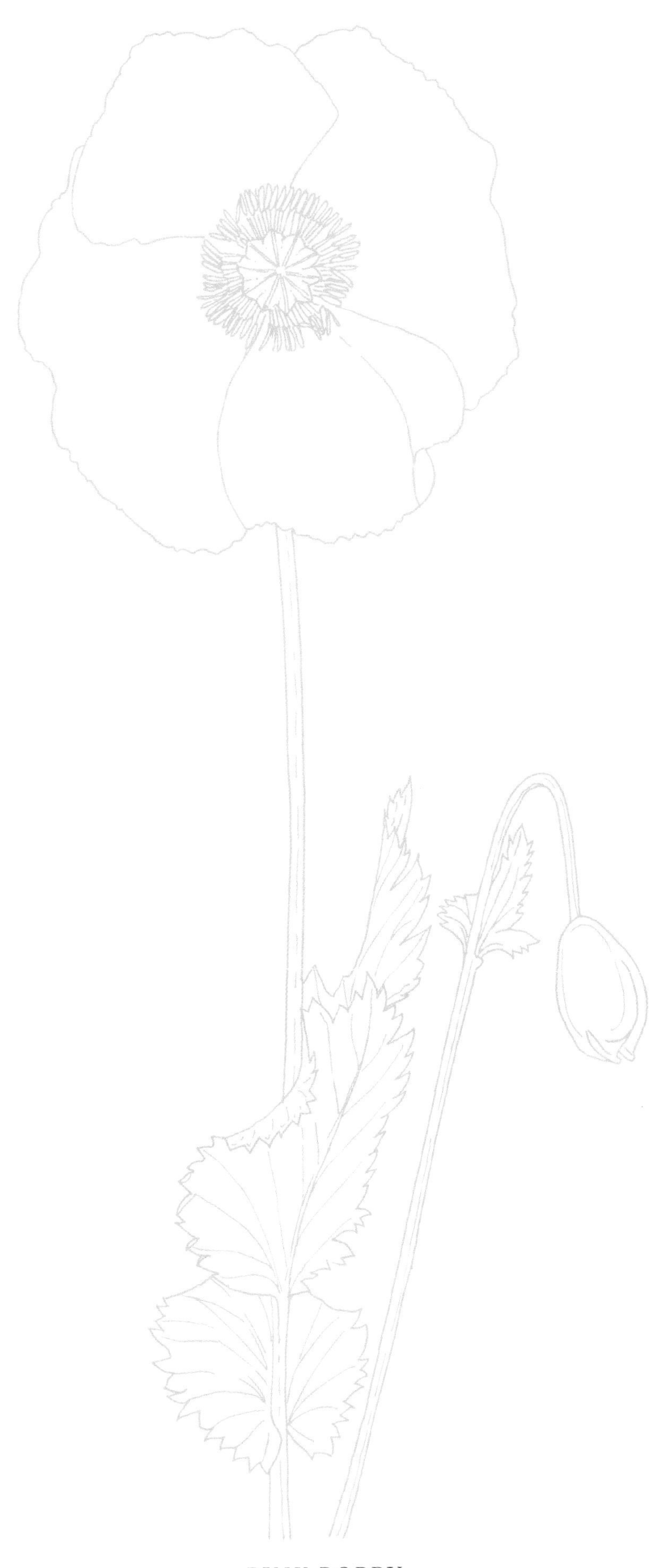

PINK POPPY

Papaver somniferum

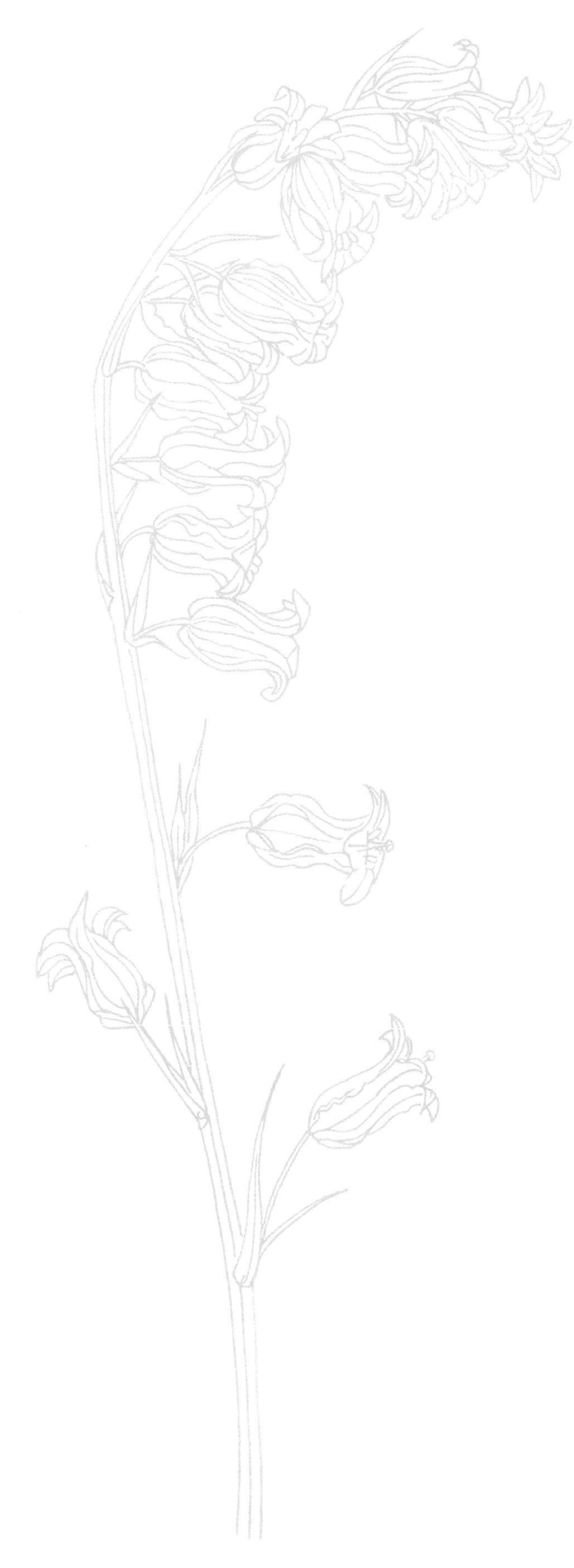

BLUEBELL
Hyacinthoides non-scripta

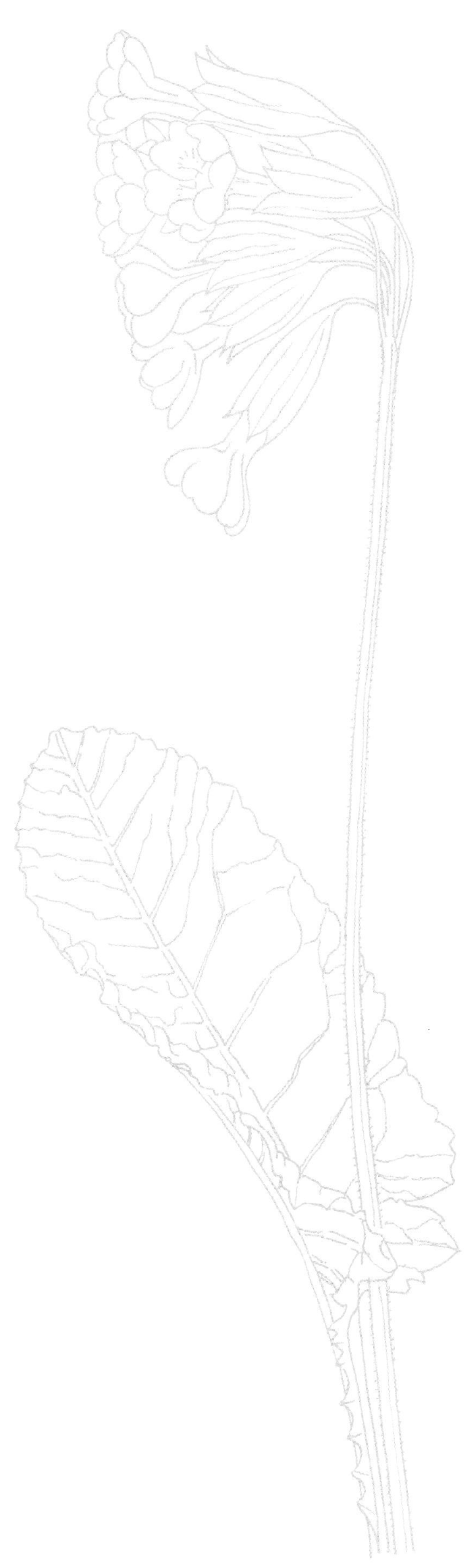

COWSLIP

Primula veris

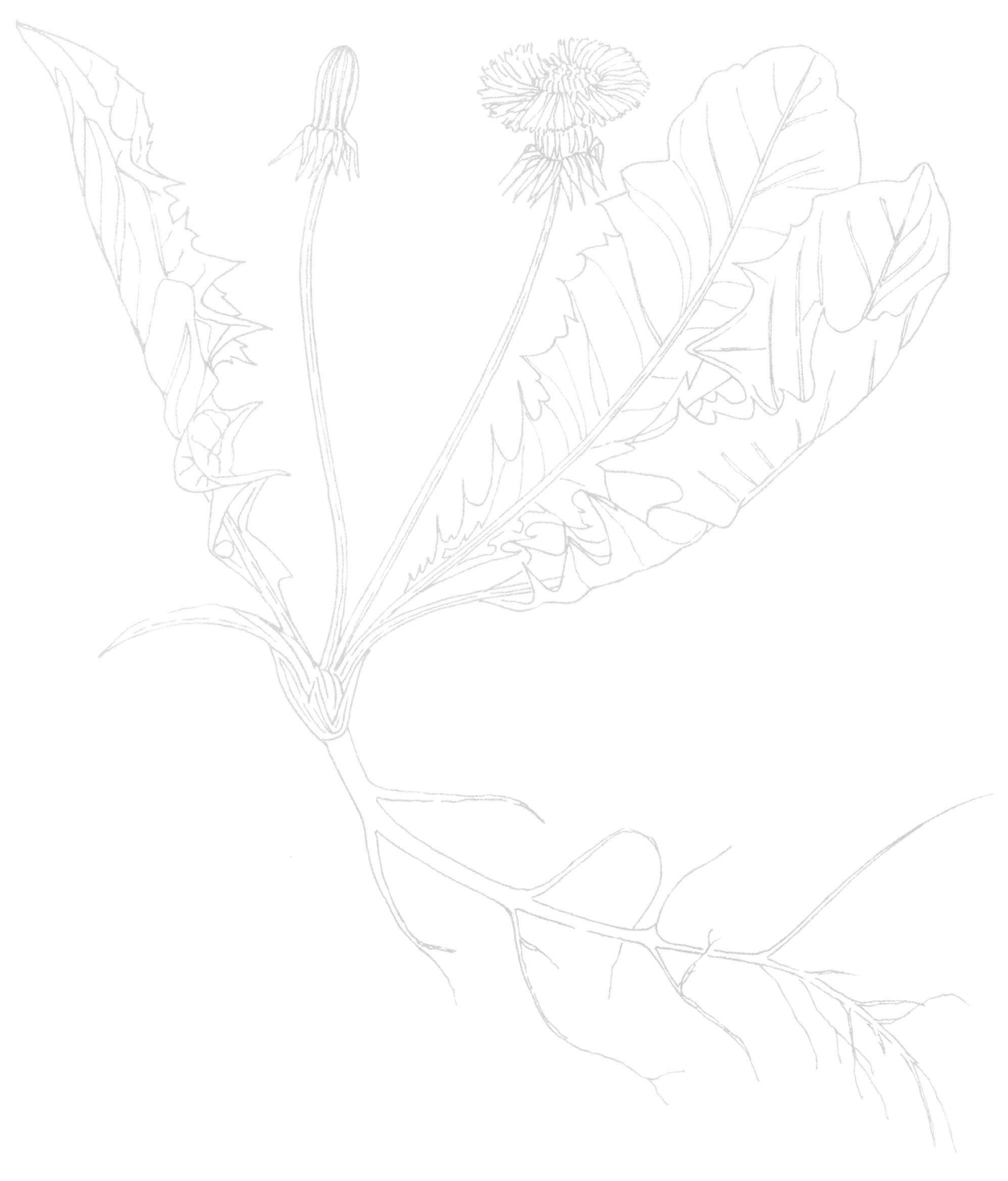

DANDELION
Taraxacum officinale